Royal Love Letters

The

Royal Love Letters

Edited by
Constance, Lady Crabtree

VIRGIN

Dedicated to
GEORGE PURVIS
who encouraged our sense of fun, and
CHRIS EDWARDS
who gave Lady Crabtree the gift of song.
There is now more laughter and music in Heaven.

First published in Great Britain in 1990 by
Virgin Books
A division of W. H. Allen & Co Plc
26 Grand Union Centre
338 Ladbroke Grove
London W10 5AH

British Library Cataloguing in Publication Data
James, Paul
    The secret royal love letters — edited by
    Constance, Lady Crabtree
    1. Humorous prose in English, 1945-   -texts
    I. Title
    828.91407
    ISBN 1-85227-260-0

Designed by Paperweight

Printed and bound by The Bath Press, Avon

PRINCESS ELIZABETH ENGAGED TO
PRINCE PHILIP OF GREECE

[text illegible]
[text illegible]

Sir Alan Lascelles, Private Secretary, September 1946.

PRINCESS ANNE TO WED LIEUTENANT MARK PHILLIPS

'It is absolute nonsense. There is no truth in it whatsoever.'

Mark Phillips, December 1972.

'There is no romance between us, and there are no grounds for rumours of a romance between us.'

Princess Anne, March 1973.

'Divorce? It has not been mentioned. By anyone.'

Princess Anne, January 1990.

DUKE OF KENT TO MARRY KATHERINE WORSLEY

'The Duke and my daughter are just good friends. A romance? Good gracious, I don't think so.'

Sir William Worsley, father of the future Duchess of Kent, 1957.

PRINCE CHARLES HAS FOUND HIS GIRL AT LAST

'Diana who?'

Constance, Lady Crabtree, September 1980.

PRINCE ANDREW WILL TAKE KOO STARK AS HIS BRIDE

'Yes, this is it this time. At last Prince Andrew has found true love. The Queen will make Andy and Koo the Duke and Duchess of Clarence.'

Morag Auchtermuchty, October 1983.

'Just two people falling head over heels in love.'

Koo Stark's agent.

Foreword

hesitantly towards the window of the Green Drawing Room, where I knew Her Majesty was posing in full evening dress for a portrait painter, I felt certain that for a split second I saw the heavy net curtains twitch. Could it have been a trick of the light, or was that momentary glint at the window really the early morning sun reflected off the Queen's familiar pearl-drop tiara? The coach backfired noisily as we turned into the Mall, and I heaved a sigh of relief as Buckingham Palace disappeared from view.

Having been relieved of my duties as relief Woman of the Bedchamber to Her Majesty in the autumn of 1988, it came as something of a surprise when I received an invitation to join members of the Royal Household staff for a day trip to France, on one of their regular social club outings. I was still a fully paid-up member — indeed it was the Queen who had encouraged me to join the club because of its weight-watchers class — and now, with time on my hands, I somewhat foolishly accepted the invitation and duly paid my deposit as commanded.

I had first entered the Royal Household in 1984 after the death of my husband, Claude, who had departed this life face downwards in the *bombe surprise* at a dinner party. It was typically inconsiderate of the man not to have waited until after the meal; as he embarrassed me in life, so he made a fool of me in death. Luckily no lasting stain was left on my double damask. Faced with astronomical death duties and the fact that Claude had not paid any insurance premiums since 1963, I think the Queen took pity on me, graciously offering me the post of relief Woman of the Bedchamber. The job carries no pay but many perks, the least of which is free banquets on duty and the best address in London. I thoroughly enjoyed the variety that the work offered, one minute popping down to the chemist's in Pimlico to buy a sinus inhaler and the next zipping the 42nd monarch since William the Conqueror into a jewel-encrusted gown for the State Opening of Parliament. From walking the corgis in Green Park to choosing a going-away card for Princess Michael of Kent, there was never a dull moment. I was part confidante, part adviser, part chiropodist.

I would probably still be in Her Majesty's service today had it not been for a quirk of fate. On the day after the Queen's 60th birthday, when we were all feeling a bit jaded (I'm positive somebody slipped something into my gin), the King and Queen of Spain made a state visit to Britain. I had been invited to a banquet at Windsor Castle, just to make up the numbers, and was feeling decidedly off-colour. I was all right until the rack of lamb arrived on the table and then I simply had to excuse myself from the table and run to the nearest bathroom. Rushing into the York Tower I pushed open the wrong door and stumbled into the Queen's Diary Closet by mistake. One side of the room was filled with red leather-bound volumes, diaries that spanned over forty years, each filled with the Queen's handwriting. I recognised the books immediately because often when I was called upon to take Her Majesty a cup of Horlicks at night I would find her sitting up in bed beside her intruder alarm, scribbling the day's events into her diary.

My discovery of Queen Elizabeth II's diaries is now legendary, and my subsequent decision to publish choice extracts was, I hoped, the ultimate service I could perform for my Sovereign. No sooner was the book off the press and selling like hot cakes in every corner of the globe, than I received a telephone call from the Queen's Private Secretary to say that Her Majesty would not be requiring my services when she attended a Service of Dedication for the roof and vault of the restored south transept of York Minster, and would I please return the silver croup-kettle I had borrowed as soon as possible. When I was not invited to Windsor that Christmas, where in previous years I had always spent Boxing Day ironing any re-usable sheets of wrapping-paper, I was certain that I had mortally offended our monarch, and if the Queen ever set eyes on me I would be clapped in irons at the Tower of London and might never see the light of day again.

Thus my great trepidation, when I joined the Royal House-

['Upset!' Morag scowled. 'Connie, she's delighted. That's the problem.'

'I don't understand,' I said.

'Well, the rest of the Royal Family are jealous because *their* thoughts haven't been made public. There's been the Duke and Duchess of Windsor's letters, then you published the Queen's diaries. They're right peeved.' Morag opened a packet of sandwiches and sniffed them suspiciously.

'There's not much I can do about that,' I said. 'I've taken enough risks.'

Morag grinned mischievously. 'Look what I found in the Duchess of York's bedroom at Balmoral.'

She handed me a packet of letters tied with a Titian-red ribbon and a large bow.

A few weeks later I was even more astonished to receive a sudden invitation to join Princess Margaret for cocktails at Kensington Palace. Confident that I would be quizzed about releasing Her Majesty's diaries for publication, I avoided drinking too much gin, but my caution was unnecessary. Princess Margaret showed me her recent holiday snaps from Mustique, we discussed the latest Andrew Lloyd Webber musical and chatted about the advantage of sling-backs, and not a single word was said about the Queen. I could not help noticing that prominently on the side table close to my chair in the large kingfisher-blue drawing-room lay a pile of letters. In the Princess's hand, the letters quite clearly began 'To my dearest darling Peter . . .'

✳

'It's a conspiracy,' I complained to Morag that evening on the telephone: 'Everywhere I go I am confronted with love letters.'

Morag's raucous Caledonian laugh echoed down the receiver. 'Look Connie, since you got sacked from the Palace you've got plenty of free time on your hands. The Queen was thrilled when you released extracts from her diaries and put her own words in print; you could do the same for the rest of the Family. They'd thank you for it.' Morag belched loudly. The smell of Glen-muchty whisky almost wafted through the telephone.

'With my contacts in the Royal Household,' she continued, 'I can get you love letters from every palace in Britain.'

'But *love letters*? They're so personal,' I protested.

'Och, the Royal Family are used to having no privacy. Anyway, so much rubbish is written about their love lives that they'd be grateful to have their own words, the truth, made public. You'd be doing them a service, Connie.'

Morag could always be very persuasive. She and I first met at finishing school in the late 1950s, at Madame Bernice's Academy of Refinement and Beauty, and struck up an instant rapport. I have never forgotten her first words to me: 'What a lovely dress you're wearing. I wonder if that style will ever come back?' Taking her lead I emerged from kick-pleats and a pussy-bow blouse to beehive hair so high that I had to duck as I went through doors, followed by a mini-skirt and white boots. My 1960s photograph album has always been a closed book to my children when I realised what an absolute fool I had made of myself in the name of fashion. Such are Morag's qualities that I did not hesitate to recommend her to the Queen and at my instigation she has become fashion adviser to Her Majesty whenever the Royal Family are staying at Balmoral Castle, and acts as part-time dresser if required. She can always be found at the Ghillies' Balls, usually selling at a discount tartan sashes that have been woven in the Auchtermuchty Woollen Mill. Although Prince Charles calls her the Old Woman of Loch-nagar, it is fair to say that Morag's influence on the Royal Family is plain; perhaps her greatest success has been with the Duchess of York. When Sarah Ferguson first began courting Prince Andrew she was a very shy girl, slim and unassuming. Quite naturally Morag saw a danger that the public might feel she was copying Diana.

'You've got to create your own style,' advised Morag, taking her to one side at the Braemar Highland Gathering. 'Why not [illegible]

[illegible] wardrobe. It was not long before I received a postcard in my friend's familiar scrawl:

POST CARD

INSUFFICIENT POSTAGE 39P TO PAY

Balmoral,
14th August 1989.
Dear Connie,
Preparations are underway for the Princess Royal's birthday. No sign of Mark Phillips again. Anne is so désolé that she's taken to the hills with an equerry, poor girl. I'll be sending you billets-doux ere long.
Love, Mo.

The Dowager Lady Crabtree,
Crabtree Hall,
Cleghorn St Percy,
North Yorkshire.

River Dee in mist.

Over the weeks that followed Morag was true to her word. Discreet brown paper packages arrived at Crabtree Hall containing copies of letters from regal lovers to royal suitors, packed with previously unpublished revelations from the courtship of couples close to the throne. Instantly I saw that this astonishing collection of correspondence was exactly what I needed to redress the balance. What I had been able to do for the Queen I could now do for the rest of the Royal Family. Combined with the letters, Morag had been able to collect a fascinating mixture of royal memorabilia — a love poem from Prince Charles to Lady Diana Spencer; Prince Andrew's cinema ticket to see Koo Stark in *Emily*; the Duchess of York's original ideas for her wedding trousseau; even a recipe for Princess Margaret's aphrodisiac cocktail. In my hands I held a unique record of royal romance; posterity demanded that I put it into print. The ease with which Morag has obtained the collection only confirms her suspicion that the Royal Family appreciates honesty.

I have not renewed my subscription to the Royal Household Social Club — the dangers are too great — but I know that future generations will thank me for the risks I have taken so far. Certainly, ever since this unique collection came into my hands, I have seen the Royal Family in a new light. Who would have thought that Prince Philip was really such a romantic old softie at heart, that Princess Diana does not think that Afghanistan is a type of cheese, or that one popular royal would actually write love stories under a pseudonym? Such are the revelations that Morag Auchtermuchty has been able to unearth. What will surprise many is that the Royal Family have human emotions. Many a time at Buckingham Palace garden parties have I seen people stare with fascination at the Queen holding a cup of tea.

'My God, she actually drinks like the rest of us . . .'

Well, yes, and she fell in love too. The only marked difference between 'us' and 'them' is that when royalty fall in love their faces appear on china mugs and tea-cloths.

When Queen Victoria first met Prince Albert in the autumn of 1839, she wrote to her uncle Leopold, 'I *may* like him as a friend, and as a *cousin*, and as a *brother*, but not *more*.' Yet, just three days later she proposed to him and within months had whisked him down the aisle. After their wedding night she

wrote, 'He is perfection in every way — in beauty, in everything
. . . Oh, how I adore and love him.' Obviously, first impressions
can be wrong, and royalty are just as susceptible today. Unfortunately they so rarely meet anyone more than once that they

actually proposed to Prince Philip in the same way that Queen
Victoria asked Prince Albert to marry her. We can only read
between the lines . . .

On 21 January 1941, Sir Henry 'Chips' Channon wrote in his
diary: 'An enjoyable Greek cocktail party. Prince Philip of
Greece was there. He is to be our Prince Consort, and that is
why he is serving in the Navy.' Princess Elizabeth was then only
fifteen, and at the time surely nobody could have known who
she would eventually marry. Or could they? Now that we have
'Mashed Potato' Morag's findings, we can see that there was
romance in the air even before the outbreak of war.

Royal romances since the war have become increasingly more
public. A list of potential brides for Prince Charles was published in 1958, yet some 22 years and 122 girls were to pass
before he found his 'Lady Di'. Princess Margaret's lovelife
appears to have been an open book, and there was many a saucy
chapter in Prince Andrew's story before he discovered 'Fergie'.
Even Prince William is beginning to cast a roving eye, obviously
only too aware of the pressures on him to find a suitable Queen
Consort. In putting together this collection of correspondence I
hope that many myths and rumours that have surrounded royal
romances will finally be laid to rest. Although Raine Spencer,
Nigel Dempster and Margaret Thatcher have pleaded with me to
include their letters, I am afraid I have been forced to restrict my
revelations to the royal mail. Contrary to popular belief, having
shared a chicken portion with Her Majesty at an informal
luncheon is insufficient to qualify for royal status.

When King Edward VIII gave up his throne to marry the

twice-divorced Wallis Simpson, theirs was hailed as the greatest love story ever told. Yet, having witnessed the Duchess of York counting her teeth after one of Prince Andrew's passionate kisses, the fond way in which the Princess of Wales commissioned the Emanuels to create an extra large pair of ear-muffs for Prince Charles's birthday, and the manner in which Princess Michael of Kent does impressions of Lucrezia Borgia at dinner just to amuse her husband, I know that there are even greater love stories to be told.

Constance, Lady Crabtree

THE ROYAL HOUSEHOLD SOCIAL CLUB

6.00 a.m. and will return in time to watch the Duke and Duchess of York's arrival in Canada on the nine o'clock news in the evening.

The Master of the Household has asked me to point out that anyone who has not completed the washing-up from the previous day's Garden Party will be unable to attend. Packed lunches will be available from the Palace kitchens at cost price. Staff, as usual, will be seated in order of seniority with Private Secretaries at the front of the coach and Pages of the Backstairs at the rear.

The Queen and the Duke of Edinburgh will be undertaking engagements in Kent for much of the day, and Her Majesty has graciously agreed to find lunch at the County Agricultural Show in Detling before travelling to Windsor for the weekend.

Will any member wishing to come on the trip please give their name to either Victor Morley-Burke (Aide de Camp) or Verona Heffer (Housemaid). A deposit of £67.22 (non-returnable) must be paid to the Keeper of the Privy Purse by 31st March.

Yours sincerely,

Hon. Sec.

The Dowager Lady Crabtree

From: Morag Auchtermuchty (Mrs)
Branch Sec. Licensed Victuallers Choir

1st October 1989

Dear Connie,

Here is the first batch of letters as promised. Once word had got out amongst the Balmoral housemaids that you were compiling another book it was not long before items began to turn up. It's amazing what you can find when you dust thoroughly. My Angus thinks he's got money stashed away, but a quick spring clean under the floorboards revealed all I needed to know. He's worth far more dead than alive, but I'm not often tempted to slip something into his cocoa. Did I tell you that he has a little car repair service on the side now? Angus Auchtermuchty was too expensive to put on a sign so he just uses his initials, AA, and it's doing very well.

My Katriona is trying that new diet of the Duchess of York's. She's down to 18 stone now. She's still auditioning for Andrew Lloyd Webber but no luck so far. I know that she caused a lot of damage on roller-skates when she auditioned for 'Starlight Express', but you'd think there would be something for her in 'Phantom of the Opera'. Ewan is still a big worry to me, Connie, but he has at last found a steady job as a chicken plucker so we're hoping to get all the poultry free this Christmas. At least he now smells better than when he was gutting fish all day.

Well, that's the news up to date. You'll be pleased to know that the Duke of Edinburgh's boils are clearing up now that he has taken my advice not to wear polyester bow ties.

Your wee chum,

Morag

which the little Princess ~~~~~~~ ~~~~~~~~~~~~~

Although Princess Margaret Rose is still a month away from her
ninth birthday, she is *extremely* advanced for her age. As her
Governess, I wonder if it is wise to take her to the Royal Naval
College where she will be surrounded by sailors? Only last
week I lost two balls of wool and was horrified to discover that
the Princess had them down the front of her blouse. Today, while
I was teaching them about Constitutional Monarchy and its role in
the Empire, Princess Elizabeth gave the work her total concentration
but Princess Margaret Rose was painting Cupid bow lips on herself
with red crayon. Could she perhaps have extra lessons while
Princess Elizabeth goes ashore?

Your humble Servant,

Marion Crawford

Royal Lodge
Windsor Great Park.

21st July 1939.

Dear Crawfie,

The Queen and I feel that Princess Margaret
Rose is a perfectly normal nine-year old girl,
and we are sure your fears are unfounded

George R

COURT CIRCULAR

BUCKINGHAM PALACE
July 23, 1939: The King and Queen, accompanied by Princess Elizabeth and Princess Margaret Rose, this morning sailed from Weymouth aboard the Royal Yacht *Victoria and Albert* to visit the Royal Naval College, Dartmouth. Their Majesties were escorted by Captain Dalrymple-Hamilton and

ROYAL NAVAL COLLEGE
DARTMOUTH

25ᵗʰ July 1939.

Dear Princess Elizabeth,

I hope that you enjoyed your weekend visit to Dartmouth? Your sister seemed to think that it was very funny when I was introduced to you as the Captain's 'Doggie', and although you very kindly fed me with biscuits, I feel that I should point out that it is a naval term for 'messenger'. I have only been a naval cadet since the 4th May, but the Captain, Freddy Dalrymple-Hamilton, is an old friend of my Uncle Dickie's, which is why I was asked to act as your escort. I expect you know what it is like being related to people in high places.

Talking of high places, I wondered if you would like to have tea with me one day in the penthouse flat that my Uncle Dickie and Aunt Edwina have in Park Lane? It is just a short distance from Buckingham Palace. I would love to show you their lift which can reach the top floor in just four seconds.

Yours hopefully,

Philip of Greece.

mumps and others had chicken pox. As we were already dressed in matching powder blue frocks (Mummy's favourite colour), my sister threatened to jump off the side of the ship if we weren't allowed ashore.

It was kind of you to be the 'doggie' and look after us, although Crawfie said that you showed off a good deal by eating so many platefuls of shrimps and an enormous banana split, and Papa called you a young fool for rowing after the Royal Yacht as we sailed down the River Dart, but my sister thought you looked like a Viking. Maybe it is your haircut.

Yes, I know all about the lift. My grandmother, Queen Mary, was once trapped inside it and was rocketed up and down for several minutes. She emerged angry but unruffled, her toque in place, her Woodbine still alight.

I would like to have tea with you, but Mummy says I am not free to do so until 1944.

Yours sincerely,

Elizabeth Windsor

WINDSOR CASTLE

To: Prince Philip Schleswig - Holstein - Sonderburg
  - Glucksburg of Greece

27th July, 1939.
Midnight, written by
torchlight.

Dear Prince Philip,

My sister Princess Elizabeth and I loved our visit to Devon, and I especially enjoyed playing with Teddy Dalrymple-Hamilton's little engine. On Saturday night papa was telling us at dinner how when he became a cadet more than half the college had mumps and he quickly caught it. I was quite amazed when we arrived to find that 30 years later the cadets still had mumps. Everyone was afraid that my sister might catch it. She could be Queen one day and has got to have lots of babies, so isn't allowed to catch mumps.

I was very impressed by the number of shrimps you ate at tea. We're not allowed to eat shrimps here in case we are sick. Mummy says that it wouldn't be right for a Princess to be sick. I would love to have tea with you at your uncle Dickie's instead of my sister, although we mustn't have shrimps. I would enjoy riding in the lift as my grandmother has had ours slowed down.

Yours truly,

Margaret Rose

WINDSOR CASTLE

29th July 1939
Up a tree in Windsor
Great Park.

Dear Prince Philip,

[illegible handwritten text]

in the lift. I don't mind if we do have
shrimps for tea.

Yours truly,
Margaret Rose
(PRINCESS)

P.S. We are going to
Balmoral Castle on August 1st.

BALMORAL CASTLE

To: Prince Philip Schleswig-Holstein-Sonderburg
-Glucksburg of Greece

8th August, 1939.
Deep in the heather.

Prince Philip,
We have arrived in Scotland a whole week
late because of some man called Hitler, and I still
have not received a reply from you. You can keep
your tea. I didn't want to ride in your lift anyway
and if you had any ideas about marrying me one
day, you can forget it. Yours sincerely,
Margaret Rose (HER ROYAL HIGHNESS
THE PRINCESS)

BALMORAL CASTLE

9th August 1939

Dear Prince Philip,

I must apologise for the letters that you have received from my sister Margaret. She is not yet nine years old, but tries to be grown-up. She always seems to want anything that I want and is very pleased with herself when she thinks she has beaten me to something. Mummy told her today that God made our bodies in such a way that we cannot pat ourselves on the back. Margaret now has a dislocated shoulder. For her birthday this month she has asked to be made Queen of Scotland, because she was born at Glamis Castle. Sometimes she is too clever for her own good. Recently Marcus Adams came to photograph us at Royal Lodge. He looked into his camera and said: 'Smile, please, and watch the little birdie.'

Margaret said, "You can drop the "little birdie" stuff. Get out your light meter and then adjust the lighting and your lens focus before you damage the sensitised plate.'

I apologise once again, and hope that you have recovered from the food poisoning. Shrimps can be dangerous.

Yours sincerely,

Elizabeth

22

HMS RAMILLIES

Indian Oc...

[illegible]

... brought from Corfu to England in an orange box across the sea. Did you know about that? As we are cousins, I wonder if we might write to each other again? Although you will not remember, we <u>first</u> met in November 1934 when you were a bridesmaid at the Kents' wedding. My family was very poor, but we did manage to give them a useful orange box as a wedding gift. I still laugh at the way your four-year-old sister seemed to appear from nowhere and pushed in front of you as you escorted Princess Marina down the aisle. My Uncle Dickie told me on that day that you were worth getting to know, and I'm sure he was right. By the way, my family call me 'Piggy' – because when I was five I opened the gate to a pigsty and dozens of pigs stampeded a tea party that the Landgravine of Hesse was giving. As I've grown older they say it stands for Philip In Glory, although on board ship they've changed it to POG (Prince of Greece)!

Yours affectionately,

Piggy Mountbatten

BIRKHALL

30th September 1939

Dear Piggy,

Thank you for your welcome letter. My family call me Lilibet, because when I was young I couldn't pronounce Elizabeth - but I'd much rather be Miss Piggy. Mummy and Papa have gone to London leaving Margaret and me here with our Governess (Crawfie) and our Nanny (Allah). Sir Basil Brookes (Bassey) is in charge of the Household and is very strict. He admonishes Margaret for biting her nails, but as she has seen Mr Chamberlain's nails all bitten off she said that if the Prime Minister can chew his so can she! I think that Mr Chamberlain might have a few more worries than Margaret, though.

Yesterday we tore up our German books and today began having French lessons with a Mrs Montaudon-Smith (Monty). At the moment we are staying at Birkhall (Birky) because it is cheaper to heat than Balmoral. We are not allowed to be idle as Queen Mary (Gan-Gan) says that we must do our bit for the war effort. I'm knitting socks for soldiers and have given up my egg ration; Margaret has opted to boost the morale of the Gordon Highlanders and visits the nearby Canadian lumber camp to help chop timber. Twice a week we have some evacuated children from Glasgow here to watch a filmshow and I'm trying to persuade Monty to teach us Glaswegian instead of French. One girl said today, 'I'm fa'in' awa' frae ma claes, an ma breeks are hingin' in wrunkles aboot me', which certainly does not sound like Mummy's English to me. Margaret understood every word, but then she has got a Harry Lauder record.

Crawfie says that the war will be over by Christmas, but I promise to write to you for the duration.

Yours,

Cousin Lilibet

obviously taking a little longer than usual to deliver the mail. Also your letters, sent to Balmoral, were forwarded to Sandringham where we spent Christmas, then to Royal Lodge and now to here. I hope this letter reaches you. I have not put your surname on the envelope this time as Mummy feels that if the Post Office see Schleswig-Holstein-Sonderburg-Glucksburg on tthe envelope they might not realise that you are fighting for us.

Well, Crawfie was wrong. The war was not over by Christmas. When Margaret confronted her, hse simply said, 'Ididn't say <u>which</u> Christmas'. Typical Crawfie, never one to admit that she's <u>wrong.</u>

As you can see ,we are now at Winsor Castle. Papa thinks we will be safe here. Mr Chamberlain wants us to go to Canada where it is safer, but Mummy says she will not let us go without her . Sne won't go without Papa, and as Papa will never leave we have to stay put. Papa wanted to write to Hitler½ as one reasonabel man ot sa another, to ask him to call off the war as it looks as if we will have to cancel Royal Ascot this yearr, there areno soldiers left to troop the Colour, and with the theatres closed there now can we possibly have a Royal Command Performance. Mr Chamberlain would n ot let Papa write, he says that Hitler isnt a reasonable man so it would be a waste of a stamp½ Sir Ulick Alexander, Keeper of the Privy Purse, keeps a close eye on our spending. Mummy is having to recycle hat feathers and sequins on her evening dreeses because of clothes rationing. Norman Hartnell has designed her a new crinoline, but it is going to cost a year's coupons.

It is very gloomy in the Castle: all the paintings have been taken ou t of their frames, chandeliers taken down, cabinets turned to the wall. It's very like visiting the Spencer family in peacetime, Mummy says. We all have to help with the blackout, but the Castle is so large that by the time we've put the last curtain up, it's daylight. We have our old rooms in the Landaster Tower. I share with Bobo,, as always, and Margaret is next door with Allah. It is so cold that we have to wear fur boots under our evening dresses because Sir Hill Child (Hilly), the Master of the Household, insists that we all dress for dinner as usual. Unfortu nately Crawfie's eyesight is poor and she wanders around the Castle for hours in the bl ackout trying to find the Octagon Room where we have our meals. The soup is cold by the time she arrives,but as the kitchens are so far away from the Octagon Room the soup is always cold, wartime or not.

I must close now as i have to knit ten pairs of socks for some Grenadier Gu ards as war work, and learn Queen Elizabeth I's foreign policy for homework. Do keep safe, dear Philip. I cannot help thinkign about the sailors we have lost. Margaret says that she too cannot help thinking about the sailors.

Yours,

Lilibet

HMS KENT

At sea!
1st June 1940

My dearest Lilibet,

It was a great thrill to receive your letter and so quickly too. It came via one of His Majesty's carrier pigeons, which made a change from tinned beef which we've had for lunch so often. I'm sure that you and Princess Margaret will be safe at Windsor Castle. It's kept many a marauder out in the past, but maybe you won't be there for long. You can tell Crawfie that the war will be over by this Christmas.

It was kind of you to send me the pair of socks in red, white and blue. Don't be offended, but both my feet are the same size. Rest assured that if I _did_ have one very tiny foot and one extremely large foot I would certainly wear them. Our Commander-in-Chief said I ought to be able to wear them as I can usually be guaranteed to put my foot in it.

Life is very boring at sea at the moment, and I'd like to see a bit more action. I'm going to have a word with my Uncle Dickie to see if he can get me ported to somewhere more exciting. Several of the men are seasick. We don't give them dinner, we just throw it straight overboard. It saves time. Fortunately I've found the perfect cure. I just put my tie on very tightly.

Take care of yourself. Don't let Margaret get into too much trouble.

Yours truly, P.

[...] [...] First Allah and Bobo got dressed in their caps and white aprons, and then proceeded to dress us. Margaret couldn't decide which dress to wear. Eventually Sir Hill Child came running to fetch us and said that if a bomb dropped on us it wouldn't matter what we were wearing. Gan-Gan (Queen Mary) does not agree and always has a tiara and fur stole on in the air raid shelter, insisting that the Royal Family must set an example. She is being evacuated to the Duke and Duchess of Beaufort's estate at Badminton because they have a more comfortable shelter than us. Ours is in the dungeons which are dark and full of beetles, with no proper bathroom arrangements. Margaret keeps jumping out of the shadows shouting 'Boo' and nearly giving Crawfie a heart attack.

Today a bomb dropped in Home Park during our mid-morning break. Margaret dropped her ginger biscuit, but was not allowed to pick it up even though it is wartime. We have been given helmets and gas masks. I wear mine as often as possible, but Margaret is discouraged from wearing hers. It is a Mickey Mouse one with a red nose and she seems to make disgusting noises with it whenever she has it on. Crawfie dislikes hers and was extremely upset when Sir Hill Child told her to take it off at dinner. She wasn't wearing it at the time. A gas chamber has been brought in here to test the masks out. Crawfie was persuaded to go in but was so cold when she came out that she stood by the fire to warm herself. The gas regenerated off her tweeds and nearly killed us all.

On Sunday I made my first broadcast for the BBC. It was with Derek McCulloch, 'Uncle Mac', and was to show other evacuated children that we know exactly what it is like. Margaret only agreed to say two words as we were not getting repeat fees. Must close as one of the Girl Guides here is going to teach us Cockney.

Yours,

Lilibet

17th November 1940

My dear P.,

Well, life goes on much as usual. Queen Wilhelmina arrived unexpectedly with no luggage except the clothes she happened to be wearing, which looked like a nightgown. Thank goodness Queen Mary wasn't here to see it. Mummy's dressmakers have fitted her out with one of her old gowns, but as Mummy is much shorter and plumper than the Dutch Queen I think she should have kept the nightgown. This morning a milliner came round with many hats for her to choose from. She sat for ages in front of the mirror trying on hat after hat. Eventually she settled for a very battered black one with a lopsided brim. 'This is perfect,' she said, 'This is the hat I'll have.' It was the very hat she was wearing when she arrived.

We have now come to terms with the war. Mummy says she can look the East End in the face now that Buckingham Palace has been bombed. I don't know why, because you cannot see that far through the hole in the Palace wall. The war has given us lots of new experiences that we might otherwise have missed. We've learnt how to wash dishes, how not to spend money, and what it is like to meet people more than once. Margaret and I have also been introduced to several children and we have clump parties with the RAF and American soldiers. We play sardines and hide-and-seek. Margaret always seems to be the hardest to find and is always at the bottom of the heap when we play sardines. She must get so squashed under all those soldiers.

Life is very different from when you were last here. So many of the staff have different jobs. Papa's piper now has to ...

This year Margaret has persuaded Crawfie to let us put on a Christmas
show in St George's Hall. It's going to be a Nativity Play called
'The Christmas Child'. I'm going to be one of the kings because
everyone felt that it would be good experience for me to wear a crown.
Margaret wanted to be the Angel Gabriel and fly in on a wire, but
Crawfie says she isn't the least bit angelic, so she's going to play
the Virgin Mary instead. What we would really like to do is a
pantomime, but Crawfie says 'Not until the war is over,' so maybe
next Christmas. We'll not need any training because being royal is an
acting job anyway.

Bacon and ham are now rationed. Papa nearly had a fit when Allah
suggested that we should all become Jewish. He is Head of the Church
of England after all. Do you get wireless programmes out at sea? We
listen to programmes in the evening, ITMA is our favourite. The Duke
of Gloucester does a very good impersonation of Rob Wilton, and
Margaret is able to take off Vera Lynn. Do you know her? She is a
young singer who has not let the war hinder her career.

Must close as we're doing racing predictions tonight. Although the
Grand National has been cancelled we're told that the Derby is still
going to be run as we always go to that. I fancy a horse called 'Owen
Tudor' as some of my ancestors were Tudors.

Take care. Love *Lilibet*

HMS SHROPSHIRE

3rd December 1940

Dearest Lilibet,

Thank you for your letter, which I was delighted to receive. It was the first time that you had signed 'Love'. As you will see, I have moved from HMS Kent to HMS Shropshire – I seem to be working my way through the counties. Yes, we do hear Vera Lynn on 'Sincerely Yours'. The lads say that the war is really a big publicity stunt by her agent. We also have a gramophone, but only one record, Gracie Fields singing 'Sally' at the Holbein Empire. It gets played incessantly and drives everyone mad. If only we could play it to the Germans, the war would soon be over.

For national security I'm not allowed to tell you where I am, but it must be one of the few places in the world where you can get sunburn on top of your frostbite. The ship is good though and has two decks, so we call her 'Canasta'! You'll have to ask your mother to explain that to you. The sailors are very refined, too. Always take their shoes off before putting their feet on the table. I like your idea of doing a pantomime. Can I be your Prince Charming?

Love, P. x

... the chance to do proper war work. Crawfie tried to register with the WRNS but when she put down her employer's name as 'Her Majesty the Queen' they declared her mentally unfit for war work. Papa insisted that she stay at Windsor Castle. 'You'd only end up cooking some old admiral's breakfast', he told her. At the Labour Exchange they asked me about my experience, so I told them about my parents' Coronation in 1937, my family history, how we use a chamber pot with VR on it in the air raid shelter, and so on. I also told them that I would like to work with corgis or horses.

As a birthday present Papa has made me Colonel of the Grenadier Guards and tomorrow the soldiers have to line up for inspection. I shall try to find fault with every one just to show that I am taking the position seriously. Tonight we have the whole cast of ITMA coming to the Castle to give a special performance. I do so look forward to meeting Mrs Mopp, Mona Lott and Colonel Chinstrap. Margaret can do an excellent impression of 'Can I do you now, sir?' and drops it into the conversation at every available opportunity. David Milford-Haven came for tea and hadn't a clue what she was talking about.

Soap has now been rationed in Britain for more than two months, but as my great-grandmother, Queen Alexandra, opened several soap factories we have enough cases in the dungeons to last until the end of the century. Queen Mary used to send a bar every Christmas to her many relatives, but that will obviously stop now. Austerity regulations have fixed the number of pleats, seams and buttonholes in women's clothes, as well as the width of hems, collars and sleeves. Fortunately we are unaffected. It is not the Royal Family's role to be fashionable, Crawfie says, so we can go on wearing the same outfits for years. The baths at Windsor Castle have been painted with a 5-inch line, the regulation depth of water, and it's certainly very nice to have that little bit extra.

I was sorry to hear that you had scarcely been transferred to HMS Valiant before it was seriously damaged in the Mediterranean, but congratulations on being promoted to First Lieutenant on the destroyer Wallace. I dare not tell Mummy as 'Destroyer Wallis' is her nickname for Mrs Simpson. I'm sure it will not be long before you change ships again, so I will be diplomatic and not say anything. Only last week a Lady-in-Waiting said something about an 'altercation', Mummy thought she said 'abdication' and now the poor woman has been banished to the Royal Mausoleum at Frogmore.

Must close as Margaret has organised a cocktail party in the cellars for some of the soldiers. Non-alcoholic, of course. We are going to learn how to do the 'jitterbug'.

Lots of love,

Lilibet

his cigars as a souvenir, I cannot for one minute believe that she smoked it. Even though the King smokes I am sure that Margaret won't when she grows up. Tell her that the family that smokes together, chokes together. I like the occasional cigarette myself, but then I'm a man.

There is never a dull moment at sea — shooting seagulls, playing water polo, and we have our own version of deck quoits using terrapins. I'm told that terrapins are an endangered species, so we have to play with them while they're still around. They make a very tasty supper dish too after an evening's sport. Maybe I'll get some leave this summer. It's been ages since I've been able to go on a stag hunt or shoot grouse.

I am enclosing a new photograph of myself at the Battle of Matapan last year. I was working the searchlights on HMS Valiant and I think the lighting in this picture is superb.

Look after yourself, Lilibet dear, and don't be too strict with the Grenadier Guards.

Lots of love, P.

WATERLOO CHAMBER
WINDSOR CASTLE

CHRISTMAS 1943

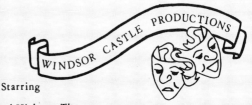

Starring

Her Royal Highness The

PRINCESS ELIZABETH
as 'ALADDIN'

& By Popular Demand

Her Royal Highness
The Princess Margaret Rose

as 'PRINCESS ROXANA'

IN

ALADDIN
and his

ROYAL LAMP

Written by

HUBERT TANNER

with additional jokes by

**HER ROYAL HIGHNESS
THE PRINCESS MARGARET ROSE**

Poster designed by

**HER ROYAL HIGHNESS
THE PRINCESS MARGARET ROSE**

Scenery constructed by soldiers of

the Grenadier Guards

with help from

**HER ROYAL HIGHNESS
THE PRINCESS MARGARET ROSE**

Costumes made by Margaret 'Bobo' MacDonald

with assistance from

**HER ROYAL HIGHNESS
THE PRINCESS MARGARET ROSE**

Tickets: 7/6d near the KING and QUEEN
   5/-   with Household Staff
   1/-   with Ordinary People

ALL PROCEEDS TO QUEEN MARY'S WOOL FUND

is very artistic. She was recently left £20,000 in the will of Mrs Ronald Greville, so has been the backer for this show. 'Maggie' Greville was always very fond of Margaret because they shared the same Christian name, but unlike my sister Mrs Greville was untouched by beauty and had a vicious tongue. She used to say that if only Winston Churchill would get permanent laryngitis, we would win the war. When my great-grandfather's mistress, Alice Keppel, escaped from France at the outbreak of war Mrs Greville said one day at tea. 'To hear her talk, one would think she had swum the Channel with her maid between her teeth.' She was, nevertheless, very kind to leave my sister money, and she did lend Mummy and Papa her country home at Polesden Lacey to have their honeymoon.

Rehearsals for Aladdin are going very well, although Papa says my tunic is too short. It isn't right, he says, for a Princess to show so much leg. Quick as a flash, Margaret told him that war-time rationing meant we couldn't get any extra material. That seemed to do the trick. Everyone will know that I'm playing the part of a boy, so they won't bother to look at my legs. I shall be wearing a pair of Crawfie's elastic support hose underneath anyway.

I am sure that you will be glad to be back on dry land again. I do feel for you at sea. Recently we went on to the set of Noël Coward's new film 'In Which We Serve' and I felt quite seasick. Margaret frequently sings Mr Coward's songs at the piano, but her choice can be very inopportune. We have a new French teacher, Madame Antoinette de Bellaigue, and no sooner had she arrived than Margaret got out the score of 'Cavalcade' and began to play 'There's Always Something Fishy About The French'. As Crawfie also calls her Marie Antoinette, the poor woman has not been made to feel too welcome. I can assure you, dear Philip, that the welcome from my family is bound to be warmer for you. Maybe there will be something to celebrate, too, as Crawfie says the war will be over by this Christmas.

With much love,

Lilibet

HMS WHELP

Back at sea!
20th January 1944.

My dearest Lilibet,

I did so enjoy spending Christmas with you at Windsor. My goodness, how you have blossomed. When I last saw you I thought of you as a child, but now you have developed into a beautiful woman. Even the elastic support hose did nothing to mar your shapely legs and thighs.

It was quite _____ nd when I saw the _____ igh kicks I really _____ specially when you _____ nd I was able to _____ nickers. It was all _____ xciting. No doubt _____ not what the King ha _____ but it certainly w _____ It made my day, I ca _____ I hope you won't b _____ or too offended.

I hope th _____ he day no matter _____ come, and it wor _____ even if I am Greek by birth.

(overlaid note:)
Dear Connie, Prince Philip is starting to get a bit too amorous here for public readership. I think that some of these should be censored.

Morag

Ps. Enclose some garlic pearlies as a gift. I'll invoice you for them later.

M

I hope that you won't be embarrassed by some of the things I have said, but I mean them from the bottom of my heart.

All my love,
P. x

HMS WHELP

P. ×××× ×××

WINDSOR CASTLE

14 February 1944

Dear Prince Philip,
    I am commanded by Her Royal Highness the Princess Elizabeth
to thank you for your letters of 31st January and 7th February.
    The Princess was most grateful for your kind thoughts and I
am to send you Her Royal Highness's best wishes.
    Yours sincerely,

Sir Alan Lascelles
Private Secretary to the King

BUCKINGHAM PALACE

Her Majesty Queen Mary,   1ˢᵀ March 1944.
Badminton House,
Badminton, Gloucestershire.

My dear Mother,

Elizabeth and I are a little concerned that Lilibet is becoming too attached to Prince Philip of Greece. He is some five years older than she and she has never met any boys of her own age. Although she has not mentioned marriage, I hear via Crawfie that it is on her mind. Our two daughters are so very different. Although still only thirteen, Margaret is very worldly and has received several proposals of marriage already. Naturally she has turned them down, this isn't China, but at least the offers have been there. Lilibet is just a little unworldly. Last week we sat her next to a professor at dinner who began to discuss the poet Dante. I was delighted to see that Lilibet was chatting animatedly in return, but suddenly the professor's face went blank. It turned out that Lilibet was discussing a horse called 'Dante' who is running in the Derby. Not such a divine comedy. Should we perhaps get her on 'In Town Tonight' or some lessons from Elsie and Doris Walters to widen her interests?

I trust you have recovered from your fall? You really should not climb ladders to remove ivy at your age.

Your ever loving son,

Bertie.

38

Thank you for your letter. Yes, of course I have recovered from my fall. We are royal. We cannot let things get us down. You must be firm with Lilibet. She is eighteen next month so start her off on the round of royal engagements. Cutting tapes, launching battleships, visiting munitions factories and meeting members of ENSA will quickly divert her energies away from thoughts of love. Why not make her a Counsellor of State or put her in one of the Women's Services, that would give her added responsibility. If all else fails, then a tighter liberty bodice and a few hours a day salvaging scrap metal for the war effort should do the trick.

Saw a photograph of Elizabeth in 'The Times'. Tell her to straighten her back and stand erect when out in public. Royalty <u>must</u> set an example in public.

Ever and aye,

Love,

Mother

18th January 1945

Dear Philip,

I am sorry that I have not written to you for so long, but I have been so very busy. Thank you for your last 127 letters, I am always interested to hear all your news. I am now doing my bit for the country and have joined the Auxiliary Territorial Service at the number one Mechanical Transport Training Centre where I am taking a complete course in driving and car maintenance. I am now officially Second Subaltern Elizabeth Windsor No.230873. I am treated like any other girl, except for a chauffeur-driven car back to Windsor Castle each evening in time for dinner and a personal detective. Oh, and a Lady-in-Waiting to hold my handbag while I strip and service an engine. Margaret was very jealous of my having a uniform, but once she realised that khaki would not complement her complexion, she calmed down a little.

Today my Aunt Mary, the Princess Royal, came to the ATS Depot at Camberley for an inspection. You've no idea how hard we had to work getting everything ready, painting walls, washing floors, tacking down red carpet. It really is such a bother when royalty comes to call. Then when I got home Mummy complained because I talked 'sparking plugs' all through dinner, so it's not been a good day.

This evening Crawfie noticed your photograph on my mantelpiece. 'Is that altogether wise?' she asked. 'You know how the staff gossip.' So I've changed it to one of you with a beard. I defy anyone to recognise you incognito.

Because we still have clothes rationing Mummy has handed some of her clothes down to me. These I will eventually pass on to Margaret. The newspapers often complain that Margaret and I seem to be

— 2 —

dressed identically. Little do they know it is often the same frock.
For my birthday this year I am to be given my own room at Windsor.

Aberdeen, George Buthlay, since last but every time she says she wants
to leave, Mummy finds a reason to make her stay. I hear that your
cousin Sandra is to marry King Peter of Yugoslavia. Mummy and Papa
received an invitation, but as it is going to be in a Greek Orthodox
Church they are going to send Princess Marina instead.

The newspapers have been cruel to Margaret again. One said that
she had such a pretty chin so has added two more. Really, it's only
puppy fat and she will soon grow out of it. Unfortunately she now
has a complex about her weight, and goes out training with local
soldiers as often as possible. She returns in good spirits, even
though many of the men are exhausted. I have passed on your message
to her about not confusing 'jitterbug' with 'doodlebug', but her
parties go with a bang anyway.

I count the days until we meet again, dearest Philip, so please
look after yourself and don't try and do anything brave. I'm sure
that your Uncle Dickie could find you a safe job at the Admiralty,
just a stone's throw from Buckingham Palace, until the war is over.

With lots of love,

Lilibet

41

BUCKINGHAM PALACE

Her Majesty Queen Mary,   8th May 1945.
Badminton House
Badminton, Gloucestershire.

My dear Mother,

At last the war is over and celebrations for
peace are all around us. It was marvellous
to take Margaret away from Windsor for the
first time in nearly five years. Now that the
war is over, one major battle looms. The question
of Prince Philip who will soon be home. Lilibet
had her first taste of champagne today and
now tells us that she is in love with Philip and
wishes to marry him. Mountbatten tells me that
Philip has already suggested that he acquires
British nationality so that he will qualify for a
permanent commission in the Royal Navy, but
even so, the future of the monarchy is in Lilibet's
hands. Will the British people really stand for her
becoming Elizabeth Schleswig - Holstein - Sonderburg -
Glucksburg? When Queen Victoria married Prince Albert
she took his name of Saxe-Coburg-Gotha, and
Father had to change it to 'Windsor' after the last
war. We cannot go through all that again.
Philip is a nice enough boy, but very ebullient with
little respect for titles and tradition. On his last
visit he pinned a notice saying 'Maggie's Playroom'
on Margaret's door, he's used ancestral portraits for
target practice, and ' over here, mush' is not how
one would address the Master of the Household.
What do you advise, Mother dearest ?
We all look forward to your return to
London and trust that you will employ a firm
of builders to repair Marlborough House and
will not undertake the work yourself.

Your ever loving son,

Bertie.

42

To HM. King George VI

Badminton House,
Badminton.

marriage under the Royal Marriages Act of 1772 which means Lilibet cannot marry before she is twenty-five without your consent. Maybe you should also point out that she is already related to him. They are third cousins through Queen Victoria, second cousins once removed through King Christian IV of Denmark and fourth cousins once removed through King George III. You only have to look at some of our dippy relations already to see what in-breeding can do.

    I have almost finished working on a needlework carpet which I am going to sell to Canada. The proceeds should help pay off some of the war debt. I shall be back in London this week and shall want to do a little refurbishing. I shall visit Buckingham Palace on Saturday as there are a few items in the Chinese Luncheon Room which would look well at Marlborough House and I'm sure Elizabeth will not mind my having the marquetry kingwood porcelain mounted Italian Renaissance walnut credenza, which would look charming in my breakfast room.

                  Ever and aye,

                    Love,

                    Mother

BALMORAL CASTLE

To: Her Majesty Queen Mary   25th August 1945

Dear Mother,

   Prince Philip has been here over a month now, but he and
Lilibet have hardly had a chance to be alone. Margaret never
gives them any time together and three really must be a
crowd. Although we've tried to treat our daughters alike,
inevitably there is sibling rivalry. Last week Margaret put
a frog in Lilibet's bed, telling her to kiss it and it would
turn into Philip. Whenever we play Charades, Margaret always
has to go one better than her sister. Last night Lilibet did
'The Seven Ages of Man', very cleverly we thought, but then
Margaret did 'The Seven Ages of Woman' - baby, child, girl,
young woman, young woman, young woman, young woman - which
even made Alice, the Duchess of Gloucester, laugh, which is
no easy thing. Elizabeth and I are planning an official
visit to South Africa which will last four months, so have
decided to take both girls along. We'll see what that kind of
separation from Philip will do.

   Your ever loving son,   *Bertie.*

WINDSOR CASTLE

MEMORANDUM

To Her Royal Highness the Princess Elizabeth.

Dear Lilibet,
    Your Mother and I feel that Philip should
be naturalised.
                    Papa   Royal Lodge

BUCKINGHAM PALACE

MEMORANDUM

To: His Majesty The King

Dear Papa,

That is very unkind. Philip and I want to have children.

                    Lilibet

HMS VANGUARD

[illegible]

[illegible] Everything seems to be against us. Throughout most of last year you were at sea, and now you are at home <u>I'm</u> at sea. First they posted you to <u>HMS Glendower</u> in North Wales, just too far to make it to London for a weekend, and when you were transferred to HMS <u>Royal Arthur</u> and were able to get to the Palace they made you eat with the Household staff. I was very excited when you told me that your naturalisation papers have come through and that you are to take your Oath of Allegiance on 29th February, but Philip, this isn't a Leap Year!

Margaret keeps trying to cheer me up by playing songs from 'Oklahoma' on the piano, but she plays <u>our</u> tune 'People Will Say We're In Love' too often. Her favourite is 'I'm Just a Girl Who Can't Say No'. Papa's equerry, Peter Townsend, is being very kind to us and always finds ways to amuse Margaret whenever I feel like being alone to think about you.

Hopefully the weather will be better when we arrive in South Africa. Apparently it is very bad in Britain. We had a letter from Crawfie saying that she had cut her face on an icicle which had formed on her sheet in the night from her own breath. It does so make me homesick for Balmoral, Sandringham, Windsor, Royal Lodge, Holyrood House and Buckingham Palace.

Have you thought of any English-sounding surnames to keep

the family happy? I'm not sure that I like your suggestion of Oldcastle. I know it is derived from one of your family's names, Oldburg, but I don't know whether I want to be Mrs Oldcastle. It makes me sound like a character from Jack Warner's Garrison Theatre. It is so frustrating now that it has been agreed that we can marry to have to keep it secret so that it does not interfere with my 21st birthday celebrations. My birthday present this year is to be a flag, coat of arms, a secretary and a lady-in-waiting of my very own. Margaret says that she would like to have a secretary for her birthday, then she could dictate words that she couldn't spell.

I shall count the days until our return to England on 11th May. It's so hard to put on a brave face. 'Where's Philip, then?' one of the sailors asked the very moment we came on board, obviously a Daily Mirror reader. 'Poor Lil,' said Margaret. 'Nothing of your own. Not even your love affair.' Sometimes being royal has its drawbacks. Nothing is private, yet we have to keep everything secret. As Margaret says, being royal means not being able to go to the lavatory when you want because everyone will know where you are.

Take care, my Prince.

Love,

Lilibet

P.S. How are the corgis? I do miss them so.

Cape Town Argus

Their Majesties King George and Queen Elizabeth, with the Princesses Elizabeth and Margaret Rose, arrived in Cape Town today. Lieutenant Philip Mountbatten RN was not with them, but is expected to marry Princess Margaret later this year. He will be King Philip I of England and an official announcement is expected to be made during this visit.

grandstands at Badminton this year.

It was so kind of you to renounce your foreign titles and take British citizenship just for me this year. I would do the same for you, but then I might end up as Queen of Greece or something. You are so, so kind to me, dearest Philip, and at twenty-one I feel that I have <u>so little</u> to offer you, with scarcely a palace or a country to call my own. You do still want to marry me, don't you?

I know that Margaret is only seventeen, but already she seems so much more mature than me. Whenever possible she smokes Queen Mary's Woodbines, and knows exactly how much water to put in the gin bottle so that nobody notices that a tot is missing. I wish that I could be as daring.

Only three months to our wedding. I do so look forward to settling down as a normal married couple. Do write soon.

Always yours,

Lilibet

Her Royal Highness the Princess Elizabeth

requests the pleasure of the company of

Lieutenant Philip Mountbatten RN

for a quiet candlelit dinner
at Buckingham Palace
on 20 October 1947

RSVP   *Dress Informal*

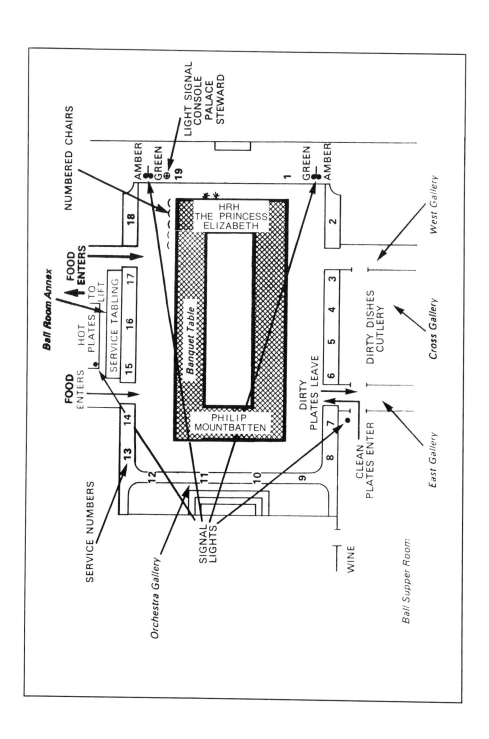

You must be there Crawfie!
Lilibet

The Lord Chamberlain is commanded by Their Majesties to invite

. . . .

. . . .

. . . .

Lieutenant Philip Mountbatten, Royal Navy

in Westminster Abbey
on Thursday 20th November, 1947
at 11.30 a.m.

Dress: Civilians – Morning Dress or Lounge Suits;
Serving Officers – Service Dress;
Ladies – Morning Dress with Hats.

An answer is requested addressed to the Lord Chamberlain,
St James's Palace, London S.W.1.

Elizabeth e Philip

You are invited to the Wedding of

.....*Miss Marion Crawford*.......

to

.....*George Buthlay esq*.....
at
Dunfermline Abbey, Fife,
on
16th September 1947.

We beat you to it!

19th November 1947

My Dearest Lilibet

In just a few hours' time you will be walking down the aisle at Westminster Abbey as a bride, and I just wanted to drop you a line to let you know that your dear Papa and I will be thinking about you and praying for you. It's so hard to believe that our own little Princess will be leaving us, but in your new home at Clarence House you will only be a short carriage drive away, and if you feel homesick for the Palace you need only look out of the window. Whenever possible I will pop on a tiara, stand on the balcony and wave.

Now for more delicate matters. As your mother, I feel it my duty to give you a few words of advice about your wedding night. This can be a terrible ordeal for a girl. However much you love Philip, never forget that he is a MAN. I cannot say whether his Greek background makes any difference, but who knows what funny ideas he might have picked up in the Navy. Do make sure that the lights are out before you get undressed, and certainly before HE gets undressed. Don't let him tie you to anything, question you about your Civil List income or make you dress up as a housemaid. My advice is to close your eyes and recite the countries of the Commonwealth.

Papa has today granted Philip royal status, and will tomorrow make him Baron Greenwich, Earl of Merioneth, Duke of Edinburgh and a Knight of the Garter - the weight of which should certainly cool his ardour.

your ever loving

Mummy

From: Morag Auchtermuchty (Mrs)

could have given the Queen a lot of useful tips. I wish she'd had some
rollers in during the ceremony her hair would have looked nice for the
reception. But she was a beautiful, virginal bride. She'd been saying
'no' to Prince Philip for so long that she almost didn't say 'I will' at
the altar. Not like your sister, Millie! How many times has she been
married now? Five? She's been down the aisle so many times they're trying
to get her to pay for the carpet.

I enclose some of Princess Margaret's correspondence. This was no easy
task, Connie, because there's so much to choose from. She may only have
been married once, but she's the royal equivalent of your sister. Princess
Margaret insists that her marriage was a happy one; it was the living
together afterwards that caused the problems. Still, they did prove Prince
Philip wrong by at least leaving the church together. Perhaps it might
have worked with Peter Townsend, but then there was the age difference. He
was at that difficult time of life when his mind wanted to join in all her
activities, but his body wouldn't let him. With Lord Snowdon there was the
problem of class — he wanted to be royal and she didn't — and with Roddy
Llewelyn there were religious difficulties. She worshipped money and he
didn't have any.

Katriona almost got a part in the musical 'Cats' this week, but perhaps
going to the audition in a Garfield costume wasn't such a good idea after
all. Ewan's got a new girlfriend, a pheasant plucker from the same factory
where he works. At least, I think that's what he said. The doctor has
told Angus to give up the cigarettes, which hasn't pleased him. Coughing
over kippers has saved a fortune in smoking them.

Take care, now.

Your wee chum,

Morag

51

CLARENCE HOUSE
S.W.1

11th June 1953

My darling Peter,

Mummy and I had an unexpected visit from Lilibet, the first time that she has visited us since we moved in, <u>and</u> since she was crowned. Obviously we've made a few changes since she and Philip lived here when Papa was alive, and Lil made it quite apparent that she did not approve. She never actually says anything, but I knew from the clucking noises that she made when she saw the small bar that Mummy has had put in the corner of the drawing room that it was not to her taste.

Fortunately, she still hasn't got wind of our affair. Mummy took it very well, considering that 'divorce' is an ugly word in her book - ever since Auntie Wallis came on the scene - and I know that she does not really like me seeing a member of staff, but she seems to be on my side and pushed the newspapers under the sofa as soon as Lilibet was announced.

She is bound to find out sooner or later, and then who knows what will happen? Until it does, who cares?

Will meet you in the Mews behind the Coronation coach as planned.

Luv ya.

Margaret.

...ress office notices what the rest of Fleet Street are saying. If only you hadn't brushed my jacket down in such a wifely way at the Coronation, right in front of a group of journalists, we might have been able to keep things secret a little longer.

Oh, my dearest Princess, how much I love you and how different you are from Rosemary. Now that my divorce from her is absolute and I am a free man again, I spend all day thinking about your beautiful qualities. How only last week when I said, 'Darling, may I kiss your hand?' you so lovingly said, 'Certainly, but don't burn your nose on my cigarette.' When I asked you if I was the first man you had ever kissed, the jokey way in which you replied, 'Maybe - your face looks familiar.' And the wonderful relationship that you have with your family. Who else but you could tell the Queen that her dress would look perfect in the blackout; some people have tact, but you always tell the truth.

Working with you all day, having to accompany you on official engagements, pretending that you are nothing more than a Princess is just too frustrating for a chap. Please break the news to Her Majesty that you want to become Mrs Townsend, she cannot possibly have any objections.

All my love,

Peter

WINDSOR CASTLE

251 Lancaster Tower
(The Powder Blue Room)

15th June 1953

My darling Peter,

Wasn't it Bette Davis in 'Now, Voyager' who said, 'Oh, Peter, Peter, why ask for the moon when we have the stars?' I've been modelling myself on her for years. Well, Lilibet has found out about us, and we might just as well be asking for the moon. I was just having my breakfast in bed yesterday morning when she burst into my room with a copy of 'The People' and thrust it under my nose. So I told her it was true, that I do want to marry you.

'But he's divorced,' she squeaked. 'You know what that means in our family.' I offered to abdicate, but she was in no mood for jokes.

'Just give me one good reason why we shouldn't get married,' I said, puffing cigarette smoke at her, which I know she hates. It reminds her of Philip in a bad mood.

Before you could say 'Up the Commonwealth' she had Tommy Lascelles in like a shot with a list: it went on and on, seventeen pages of it. I glanced through and said, 'Yes, but have you any good reasons why we can't marry?' That took the wind out of her sails. She went off for a gallop through Home Park, but it was not long before a copy of the Royal Marriages Act of 1772 was slipped discreetly under my door.

Lilibet did not raise the matter for the rest of the day, but when we played Charades in the evening I did a Priestley play called 'When We Are Married', quite deliberately, so she did 'All the Nice Girls Love a Sailor'. Dear Mummy, of course, did Anderson's 'Tea and Sympathy'. Lilibet decided to have an early night when I started to sing songs at the piano, making her exit as I sang 'Can't Help Lovin' Dat Man O'Mine'.

As your mother, dear sweet Gladys, does not object to our relationship, I don't see why my family should. Don't worry, my darling, everything will resolve itself. I think Lilibet is probably only stalling because she wants me to babysit with Charles and Anne for the six months that she is on her Commonwealth tour. Never mind: 'while the cat's away', as they say.

Chin up!

Love, Margo

P.S. Maybe if I suggest knighthoods for certain newspaper editors in the next Honours List we might be able to stave off criticism.

... school.
... give up cigarettes.
... lcohol.
... when you're 60 he'll be 76.

He is a member of staff <u>and not royal</u>.

146/ As a divorcé he cannot marry in church.

147/ As a member of the Royal Family you cannot marry in a Registry Office.

148/ He is ex-Air Force and would never get used to walking three paces behind you.

149/ He is useless at playing charades.

150/ He has two children, and you may have once played Cinderella but you're too young to be a stepmother.

151/ Prince Philip likes to feel that he is head of the family and could never accept you marrying someone older than him. Also the Group Captain has more hair than Philip and is therefore a threat to his masculinity.

152/ The newspapers are anticipating your marriage. We are royal. We cannot be dictated to by the press.

153/ You cannot marry this year as it would overshadow news reports of our forthcoming Commonwealth Tour.

154/ You must think of Mummy, she would get so lonely at Clarence House without you, left by herself with six corgis and only 73 staff to talk to.

155/ There are so many eligible European Princes available - I managed to find one - so why do you have to choose a commoner?

WINDSOR CASTLE

15th June 1953

My dear Margo,

We were so sorry that you had to leave Windsor suddenly yesterday. I understand your concern, but would it not have been easier just to have telephoned Clarence House to see whether or not you had left your bedroom window open? We missed you at the Garter Ceremony and Mummy hopes that you will return in time for Lady's Day at Ascot as she has an accumulator bet in your name.

I know there were tensions on Sunday, dear sister, and I don't want you to think I am deliberately destroying your future happiness, but I must consider what Uncle David and Auntie Wallis would say if I let you marry a divorced man. He had to give up the throne because she had divorced Mr Simpson. What a sacrifice that was. He might want to claim the throne back again if I allow you to wed a divorcée, and we've only just had our bedroom at Buckingham Palace re-gilded. Remember what Gan-Gan would have said if she'd been alive - DUTY. I always have to think that throughout every aspect of my life and constantly have to remind Philip.

I do want you to be happy, but you must see the parallels with 1936.

Love,

Lilibet

CLARENCE HOUSE
S.W.1

16th June, 1953

Dear Lil,
Wallis Simpson had been divorced TWICE. Peter has only been divorced ONCE. So our situation is completely different.
I shall look in my diary to see if I am free for the races.
Love, Margo

I hope this has been helpful. My blessings and prayers go with you.

God bless, ✝ Geoffrey Cantuar

WINDSOR CASTLE

Nursery
17 June 1953

Dear Arnty Margo,

Nanny and Mispy say that yoor in love. Yipee! Can I be a page boy at yoor weding? Can Spike Milligan be yoor best man?

Luv

Charles xx

WINDSOR CASTLE

17th June 1953.

Dear Margaret,

As your brother-in-law I hope that you can now look upon me as one of the family, as the brother you never had. (In which case, I would be King, but we won't go into that...) Come on, old sport, you must know by now that this Townsend business just isn't on. Lilibet is right, you know, and is only trying to stop you making a complete ass of yourself. Townsend is a nice enough bloke, but the cut of his jib just isn't right. Say you married him, what would happen? At Ascot you'd be one side of the Royal Enclosure and he'd be the other, out in the grandstands with the other divorcees, bankrupts and ex-convicts. How could we have him in the carriage procession at the Derby? Stop the carriage just before entering the Royal Enclosure so that he could get out? It's just not cricket.

Give him up, Margaret. Your flame attracts plenty of other moths. Lilibet has enough headaches under the weight of the crown without her only sister adding to them.

Truly. Philip.

58

record 'Saucy Songs from Sophie' so that you
can do some more impressions. I hear ya
dropped the 'Rose' from your name,
Is that because you've been defleowered?

Look, the papers over here are having
a field day about you and this
Townsend guy. You know what I
always say, If he's good enough to
fight for this country he shouldn't
have to fight over you — so don't stand
any nonsense from the family. Look
at me. I'm on husband number three,
but if I'd listened to their families
I'd still be a virgin. Sorry, had to stop
for a laugh there. You're a bright
kid so if you want him, you have him,
girl! He's nearly forty, so what.
life begins at forty.

    Keep smilin' honey,

       Sophie Tucker

CLARENCE HOUSE
S.W. 1

22nd June 1953

My dearest darling Peter,

The world and its wife have been writing to me over the last
few days to give me advice. As if it were any of their business.
The only person who hasn't been going on at me is Mummy, who
always hopes that if she ignores a situation it will go away. If
it doesn't go away of its own accord a few nips of gin usually
help, and a game of rummy can do wonders for her morale. I wish
that our situation could be remedied so easily. Oh, I do wish
other people wouldn't interfere, it's hard enough to cope alone.

I'm afraid I've put on another stone in weight, but I always
turn to food when I'm unhappy. Thank goodness this is Coronation
year and I'm being invited to so many banquets.

Sorry that I spent most of the evening dancing with Johnny
Dalkeith and Billy Wallace at the Tennants' party last week, but
it wouldn't do for us to be seen together just at the moment. In
just eight days our official visit to Rhodesia begins and I've
made sure that you will be part of the entourage, having convinced Mummy that you are an essential member of the team.
After all, it's the Comptroller who sees to her little comforts,
organising the refreshments, lending an arm when she wobbles on
her platform soles, putting on a white glove and waving from
the window whenever she gets tired. Fortunately she now has a
new hobby. My friend, Raine McCorquodale, has a novelist for a
mother. Her name is Barbara Cartland, and Dickie Mountbatten
(Philip's uncle) introduced her to us. Mummy had always wanted
to write romantic novels, but obviously can't publish books as
Queen Mother, so they have come to an arrangement that Mummy

[illegible] with a Group Captain. 'No, too far-fetched,' she said.

Last week I went into the drawing room and saw Mummy and Barbara Cartland stooped over a manuscript. Both happened to be wearing pink chiffon and it was hard to tell who was who.

I shall count the days until we are together in Rhodesia. Lilibet has seen Lascelles, Churchill, the Privy Council and even a clairvoyant, but they will not be able to part us.

All my love,

M.

BUCKINGHAM PALACE

INTERNAL MEMO   To: Her Majesty Queen Elizabeth II
                From: Sir Alan Lascelles, Private Secretary

22-6-53

Your Majesty,
I have been planning Princess Margaret's official programme of engagements
for the next year, which should keep her away from Peter Townsend.
Out of sight, out of mind, Ma'am.

30 June - 17 July   Official visit to Rhodesia accompanying Queen
                    Elizabeth the Queen Mother. Peter Townsend will not
                    be required.

        18 July   Rest day at Clarence House - Peter Townsend will
                    be at Windsor.

   19 - 24 July   Tour of the West Midlands.

        25 July   All day visit to a coal mine.

        26 July -
     September   Princess Margaret will be in Scotland making
                    arrangements for the Queen Mother's birthday, Princess
                    Anne's birthday, and her own birthday, can organise
                    the annual Ghillies' Ball, and help with the Women's
                    Institute Bazaar in Crathie Church Hall.

  17 September   Visit to hot-air balloon factory in Bradford. Her
                    Royal Highness will be offered as many free flights
                    as possible.

  18 September   A full day of engagements in Cornwall.

> *I think a much simpler solution
> would be to send Peter away
> for a year! E II R*

  22 November   Princess Margaret will join the six month Commonwealth
                    tour. Return 15 May, 1954.

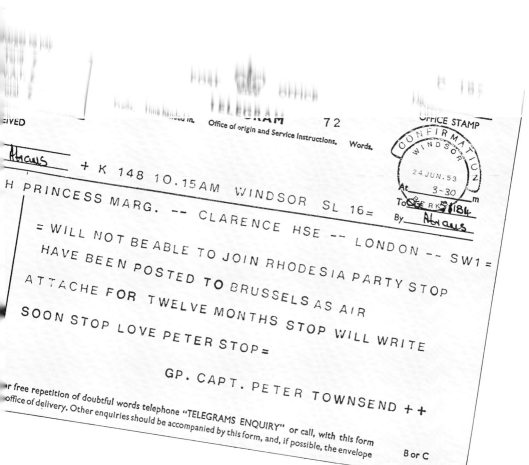

POST OFFICE TELEGRAM

Office of origin and Service Instructions.   Words.   72

RECEIVED

Angus

+ K 148 1O.15AM WINDSOR SL 16=

H PRINCESS MARG. -- CLARENCE HSE -- LONDON -- SW1 =

= WILL NOT BE ABLE TO JOIN RHODESIA PARTY STOP HAVE BEEN POSTED TO BRUSSELS AS AIR ATTACHE FOR TWELVE MONTHS STOP WILL WRITE SOON STOP LOVE PETER STOP=

GP. CAPT. PETER TOWNSEND ++

OFFICE STAMP

CONFIRMATION WINDSOR
24 JUN.53
At 3-30
To CLERK 51184
By Angus

For free repetition of doubtful words telephone "TELEGRAMS ENQUIRY" or call, with this form office of delivery. Other enquiries should be accompanied by this form, and, if possible, the envelope   B or C

Umtali.

POST CARD

My darling P.   8 - VIII - 53.
We've undertaken 54
engagements, had a welcoming
ceremonies, 28 presentations
of dignitaries, inspected
12 Guards of Honour. Have
now contacted Bulawayo
'Flu. There is only one
place this can be cured.
Belgium. Send plane
immediately.
        Love, M.

Group Captain Peter Townsend

2116 Avenue Louise

BRUSSELS

Belgium

Vumba Mountains, Rhodesia.

The British Regency Act of 1937 has been amended so that the Duke of Edinburgh will act as Regent if anything should happen to the Queen before Prince Charles reaches maturity. Princess Margaret, already pushed down to third in line to the throne, has been excluded from the Act. Sources close to the Palace say that Her Majesty's aides are concerned that Group Captain Peter Townsend could end up on the throne.

Dearest Peter,
    Now the law is against us! I didn't want to be Queen anyway, but that's not the point. It's a conspiracy. While I was away in Rhodesia the corgis were trained to ignore me. Even the piano has gone out of tune. I'm fed up.
        Love, M.

[...] with me get married?
Love, Margo

BUCKINGHAM PALACE

6th July 1954

My dear Margo,
The Privy Council decided that you must spend a year apart. They didn't say <u>which</u> year, but I'll find out.

Hope your cough is better? At night when it is quiet, if the wind is in the right direction we can actually hear you. 'Margaret's at it again', says Philip grumpily. He hates to have his sleep disturbed. Bobo is sending you some goose grease to rub on your chest, she swears by it.

Love,

Lilibet

Avenue Louise,
Brussels.

My dearest Margaret,   10th July 1954

Just a quick note, I will write more later,
but I wanted to tell you the good news. I will
be flying home to England for good on 2nd
February, next year. It will soon pass, my
darling.

                        Love,
                          Peter

BUCKINGHAM PALACE

                                              11th July 1954

My dear Margo,

The Privy Council have not yet made up their mind (there are over 300
members) but I have some marvellous news which I know will thrill you.
I've arranged for you to go on an official tour, starting on 1st February,
visiting Trinidad, Grenada, St Vincent, Barbados, Antigua, St Kitts,
Jamaica and the Bahamas. I know how you hate the British winter and will
relish the thought of getting away to the sun for a few months.

                        Love,

                          Lilibet

Buckingham Palace and I tried to get Papa to have your head chopped off. So many happy memories since then - dry martinis and wet kisses, shopping in disguise in Harrods and being mistaken for Elizabeth Taylor and Michael Wilding, and that time when we danced incognito at the '400' Club and it was so crowded that we had to do the rhumba up and down instead of sideways...

Lilibet's having a last-ditch attempt to pair me off with someone 'suitable'. I had invited Dominic Elliot, the Earl of Minto's son, to be my escort - he knows the score - but arrived to find Patrick Plunkett, Colin Tennant, Johnny Dalkeith, Sunny Blandford, Billy Wallace, Tom Egerton, Julian Fane, Mark Bonham-Carter, Michael Tree, Prince Henry of Hesse and King Michael of Rumania, all waiting, and each thinking that I only had eyes for him. Even Simon Phipps, Joyce Grenfell's cousin, was here in his dog collar (he's now a chaplain in Coventry) and I was convinced he would start a marriage ceremony at the drop of a hat. When any of them asked me did I want a drink I didn't dare say 'I do' just in case it was misconstrued. What a hoot! There are even 300 press photographers camped outside the gate, confident that some kind of announcement will be made on my birthday. Oh, to be in such demand!

Although Lilibet has got my engagement diary so full that I hardly have time to breathe, I thought perhaps we might have a May wedding, between the Derby and the Trooping the Colour, when there's a bit of a lull. What do you think?

Take care. You can send me some more of those Belgian chocolates!

All my love,

M

BALMORAL CASTLE   23rd August, 1955

My dearest darling Peter,

I'm terribly depressed and felt that I must write to you.
I may be twenty-five and in theory free to marry
who I like, but the reality is different. Sir Anthony
Eden came to Balmoral as all Prime Ministers do
once a year, only to tell me that the Cabinet
still does not agree to our union. The old hypocrite!
He's been divorced himself, how can he bang on about
the morality of it all. The Marquess of Salisbury
has even threatened to resign. All it takes is a
silly little Bill to be passed by the Government and
we can be wed. Oh how I sympathise with Auntie
Wallis now. Oh how I HATE being royal. I wish
I wasn't a Princess and how i would dearly love to
give up the whole charade and go and work in
Woolworths.

                    All my love,

                         M.

Well, as Gan-Gan would have said, 'things have come to a pretty pass'.
To-night Philip and I had our feet up and were watching Sunday Night At The
London Palladium on the television (we like to see if we can spot who is sitting
in our box) when a comedian actually said 'Tinker, Tailor, Soldier, Group
Captain'. Three guesses as to whom he was referring to. When the Royal Family
become the butt of comedians' jokes it really is too much. Is nothing sacred?

We've decided, therefore, that you CAN marry Peter Townsend. Of course
there are conditions, but the course of true love never did run smooth.

1/ You must give up your rights of succession. (This will not affect you
anyway.)

2/ You must give up your Civil List income. (Two can live as cheaply as one,
they tell me.)

3/ You must give up your title of Princess. (You want to be 'Mrs' anyway.
That's what this is all about, after all.)

4/ You must give up the jewels you have on loan. (You won't be able to afford
to go anywhere that a tiara is worn.)

I hope that you'll be happy now that at last you have exactly what you
wanted.

God Bless.

Love,

Lilibet

CLARENCE HOUSE
S.W.1

I would like it to be known that I have decided not to marry Group
Captain Peter Townsend. I have been aware that, subject to my
renouncing my rights of succession, it might have been possible
for me to contract a civil marriage. But mindful of the Church's
teaching that Christian marriage is indissoluble, and conscious
of my duty to the Commonwealth, I have resolved to put these
considerations before others.

Margaret

31st October, 1955

BUCKINGHAM PALACE

1st November 1955

Your Majesty,

Have you decided which member of the Royal Family will be attending

the premiere of <u>Rebel Without a Cause</u>?

Absolutely.

*I think Princess
Margaret would be
the most appropriate.*
EⅡR

Beechwood,

is only three years older than me, I do hope that isn't too much; he's heir to a seven-figure family fortune (enough?); his grandfather was Sir Edwin Lutyens (he designed the Cenotaph in Whitehall and Gran. Gan's doll's house); he was educated at Oxford, has a manor house in Sussex and a flat in Mayfair and has met Mummy at Newmarket, Epsom, Ascot and Goodwood, is boringly, boringly English, and has never been DIVORCED. Alright?

Margo.

BUCKINGHAM PALACE

My dear Margo,   2nd November 1955

Please don't be bitter or sarcastic, you don't want to turn out like Auntie Wallis. We would be very happy for you to marry Billy. A charming young man, just like a P G Wodehouse character, and very suitable.

Love,

Lilibet

71

CLARENCE HOUSE
S.W.1

5th November 1955

Dearest Lilibet,

I have decided <u>not</u> to marry Billy Wallace. Would you believe he's gone off to the Bahamas with Jocelyn Stevens, Andrew Craig-Harvie and Tommy Sopwith, to celebrate the end of his bachelor days. What a cheek, leaving me behind when he knows how much I love the sun. If he can leave me in foggy England now, what's it going to be like when we're married? I just know that I shall be left on the shelf now. Dishy Mark Bonham-Carter's gone and married Condé Nast's daughter, Leslie. (Yes, Les<u>lie</u>!) Colin Tennant is engaged to Lady Anne Coke. Henry Porchester married Jean Wallop, the Earl of Portsmouth's niece, and Peter Ward's married Claire Baring. I'm beginning to feel that I'm always the bridesmaid, never the bride. Even Danny Kaye is spoken for.

Please don't feel guilty, Lilibet, that because of you I shall spend a lonely life, the spinster of Clarence House.

Your loving, lonely sister,

Margo

P.S. Can't see you tomorrow as I'm going to the '400' Club with Gerald Bridgeman (the Earl of Bradford's cousin). Oh, and the day after I'll be at a Duke Ellington concert, (he's not a <u>real</u> Duke), but will see you at Royal Lodge at the weekend - or will it be Remembrance Sunday, I forget. I've also been invited to a Count Basie concert (he's not a <u>real</u> Count, either!).

ANTONY ARMSTRONG-JONES

20 Pimlico Road

I so much enjoyed meeting you at Lady Elizabeth Cavendish's dinner party last evening. It made such a change to meet a woman who isn't taller than me - no disrespect intended, Ma'am. I realise that we had all consumed large quantities of whisky, but after we had finished the hokey-cokey, you did say that you would like me to take some pictures of you. I wondered, therefore, if you would care to visit my darkroom? It's just a stone's throw from Buckingham Palace and is an old pawnbroker's (the balls are still outside) between the Sunlight Laundry and an antique shop.

I did enjoy your impression of Gracie Fields after supper and I'm sure that not many members of the Royal Family can hit an F above high C, not from under a table anyway.

I hope to hear from you again, Ma'am, and I remain your obedient servant,

Tony Armstrong-Jones.

CLARENCE HOUSE
S.W.1

24th February 1958

A. Armstrong-Jones, Esq.,
20 Pimlico Road,
London S.W.1.

Dear Mr. Armstrong-Jones,

Thank you for your letter of 21st February, addressed to Princess Margaret.

I'm sorry to have to tell you that Her Royal Highness has no recollection of you. Or the party. Or Lady Elizabeth Cavendish.

Yours sincerely,

Adam Gordon

Comptroller to Queen Elizabeth
The Queen Mother

took. I'm sure you must remember photographing me
on that occasion and I would be happy to grant
you the privilege of a visit to your studio as I am
contemplating a new portrait to be released on
my birthday. I've had my hair cut, and
rather fancy a Marilyn Monroe type pose.

     Yours sincerely,

       Margaret.

ANTONY ARMSTRONG-JONES
PHOTOGRAPHER

20 Pimlico Road
London sw1

21st March, 1958

Dear Miss Windsor,

I'm afraid I have no recollection of you.

     Yours, Tony Armstrong-Jones.

CLARENCE HOUSE
S.W.1

22nd March 1958

My dear sister Lilibet,

I think I'm in love! This is it at last. Do you remember the photographer who took pictures of Charles and Anne in 1956, the one the Duke of Kent recommended? Well, I had a sitting with him yesterday. We had corresponded so I just called in unannounced only to discover that he is such an imaginative and creative man. The poses he suggested for me are quite revolutionary and so unlike those of any past photographers we've had; His equipment makes Beaton's look like a Box Brownie, I can tell you. He would love to photograph you for Jocelyn Stevens's magazine 'Queen' - which is quite appropriate, you must admit - and visualises you dressed as Britannia. Your head is on one side of our coins, so he thinks it would be a novel idea to picture you dressed like the other side. I've seen some of his other work. He's just photographed a research chemist, recently called to the Bar, I believe (tell her mine's a double Scotch!), called Margaret Thatcher, and she looked marvellous in a Boadicea costume. There was a sixteen-year-old Welsh boy with a mop of ginger hair, Nigel Kinnock, I think, dressed as a daffodil for St David's Day. His imagination is so fertile.

He's such a handsome young man, practically the same age as me, and even my height. All my old flames - Peter, Sunny, Dominic, Johnny, Colin and Billy - are all over 6 feet. He calls me 'Ma'am' all the time and he has never been divorced. Because he is a photographer nobody will think he's interested in women, so if I'm seen in public with him everyone will think he's simply part of the press contingent. Clever, eh?

Lots of love,

Margo.

P.S. I won't be able to join the house party at Windsor this Easter as Tony wants to take me to a little flat he has in Rother-hithe to show me some of his photographs.

Tony sounds very suitable, especially if we can get official photographs at a discount which will save a large portion of the Civil List, but please don't rush into things. Philip and I have known each other nearly twenty years and I still discover unexpected aspects of his character. When he said he had a polo fixation, I had thought he meant that he liked mints, I had not realised that he would spend every weekend on horseback.

Neither did I think that his humour would be in the worst possible taste. When his mother became a nun, he told her that it shouldn't become a habit (she didn't get the joke either), and I was so embarrassed when he told the Commissioner of the Metropolitan Police that some of his force couldn't even find an elephant with a nosebleed in the snow.

Play it cool with Tony, and make sure that when he takes a photograph it isn't an exposure.

Love,

Lilibet

CLARENCE HOUSE
S.W.1

5th April, 1958.

My dear Tone,

I did so enjoy my visit to your flat in Rotherhithe Street and I do like the artisan decorations. So very different from the palaces I'm used to. What a surprise not to have curtains at the window, but as you say - it's a shame to spoil the view and I presume that only the swans on the river can look in. In fact it was a simulation to me. How daring of you not to dress for dinner, and how clever to do all your own washing up, it reminded me of being in the Girl Guides. I do like the way you call me 'Pet', too. I usually tell friends to call me 'M' - they think it is an abbreviation of Margaret, but it's a way of getting them to call me 'Ma'am' without realising it. Ingenious!

Thank you for the lovely dinner. We don't have sausages at Clarence House since Mummy nearly choked on a bone inside one, and we've not had chips for many years. The last time was during the war at Windsor when the kitchen staff tried to peel potatoes in the blackout. I hope that you will come and have a meal with us soon. My sister is having the last presentation of debutantes at court soon (between you and me I think Prince Philip enjoys them too much) and is replacing them with informal lunches at the Palace. So I'll try and get you an invitation. Such ordinary people are to be included that you'll feel quite at ease.

Your pet,

Margaret.

78

2116 Avenue Louise,

...the daughter of Franz Jamagne, a Belgian
cigarette manufacturer. An extremely nice man, I could perhaps
get you samples of his merchandise. Not being royal, her
family are not concerned about my divorce. The wedding will be
in Brussels on 21st December. I hope you can come.

Yours affectionately,

Peter

Group Captain Peter Townsend an... ...d Marie-Luce Jamagne
are to be m... ...*arried on*
21st Decemb... ...**er 1959**

and would be pleased if yo... ...*would be present*
The ceremony will ta... ...*ke place in*

St Margaret's Chu... ...ch, Brussels

R.S.V.P.

BALMORAL CASTLE   5th October, 1959.

Dear Lilibet,

I hope that you had a safe journey back to London.
Did you see the first photographs of the back of the
moon on television, taken by Luna III? Tony has
proposed to me today and I have agreed to marry
him, subject to your approval.

Love, Margo.

BUCKINGHAM PALACE

My dear Margo,   6th October 1959

We have no objection to your marrying Tony, although I was not happy
to hear recently that his father, Ronald Armstrong-Jones, has just divorced
for the <u>second</u> time. I just hope that Tony hasn't inherited all of his
father's qualities. It would be so embarrassing if you and Tony were ever
to divorce. Philip says to tell you that marriage is the chief cause of
divorce in this country.

I do have to make <u>one</u> condition. The announcement of your engagement
cannot be made public until after the birth of my baby next February. I'm
sure you won't mind waiting, you've waited long enough already, but as he
or she will be third in line to the throne (your place actually) we don't
want the event eclipsed by your engagement - especially as you will be
marrying a commoner. Protocol is <u>so</u> important.

Your loving sister,

Lilibet

baby are doing well.

CLARENCE HOUSE
S.W. 1

* * * 26th February 1960 * * 11.00 a.m. * * *

It is with the greatest pleasure that Queen Elizabeth The Queen
Mother announces the betrothal of her beloved daughter The Princess
Margaret to Mr. Antony Charles Robert Armstrong-Jones, son of
Mr. R. O. L. Armstrong-Jones, Q.C., and the Countess of Rosse, to
which union The Queen has gladly given her consent.

CLARENCE HOUSE
S.W.1

29th February 1960

My dearest Tone,

I am so glad that at long last our engagement has been made public.
No more secrecy, no more smuggling you into Clarence House disguised
as a barrel of brown ale, no more dancing at clubs every night with a
different man just to keep the press off the scent. What a relief!
Just one more hurdle to cross. Lilibet's husband was made a Duke on
their wedding day, so I want you to be made a Duke also. She surely
cannot deny me that. I think the 'Duke of Ben Nevis' would be nice as
it's the highest mountain in the British Isles, and I was born in
Scotland. I'll have a word with Lil when the fuss has died down over
her latest baby.

They've decided to call the child Andrew after Philip's father.
Uncle Henry, the Duke of Gloucester, came to see the baby today, but
his eyesight is bad and he had to peer right over the cot to see which
end was which. 'It has its mother's eyes and its father's nose,' he
said. I thought, if you lean any further over the cot it's going to
have your teeth, but I didn't say anything.

Just one thing, Tony, sweetheart. I know you won't mind my mention-
ing it, but when we first appeared in public at the Royal Opera House
for the gala ballet performance you should have let Mummy go in first,
and you should have walked <u>behind</u> me. I know that the public are
interested in seeing you, but I do rank above you. I'm fourth in line
to the throne now. Also, Tony, it was just a little embarrassing when
you started taking photographs from the Royal Box. People take pictures
of us, not we of them. You must learn to act as if you're royal, even
if you're not.

All my love,

Margo

MRS JONES.   *Tony.*

CLARENCE HOUSE
S.W. 1

2nd March 1960

Dear Tony,

    If that's your attitude, you can forget it. I'm returning your
engagement ring. You'll find it in a box marked 'GLASS – HANDLE
WITH CARE'.

                    Margaret.

Dearest Pet,   **BUCKINGHAM PALACE**   3rd March, 1960.

I'm sorry, I'm sorry. I love you and adore you's promise
to accept a title & will always walk 3 paces behind you.
You know I worship the ground your Sister reigns over. Please
accept the ring back. I'm sorry if it makes your finger go
green, but it's the most fashionable colour this year.

All My Love, Tompkins. X X X X X

CLARENCE HOUSE   4th March, 1960.
S.W.1

My dear Tony,

Thank you for your apology and I accept it. It's fun
to fight, because then we can kiss and make up. I will
still marry you, even though Mummy says Friday is
the unluckiest day to marry on, and Auntie Alice of
Athlone has written to Mummy to say "Marry in May
and rue the day", and most of my friends feel
that ours is an ill-fated match because royalty
and commoners cannot mix. Oh, and astronomers
say that Pisces and Leo are totally incompatible
because Pisceans need time alone and Leos like me
need people around them. What rubbish! We'll
prove them all wrong. See you at the Frys' house at
Broadchalk next weekend, but do remember
to arrive early. Nobody must arrive after a Princess.
All my love,

M. xxxx

The Duke of Edinburgh PHILIP
The Heir Apparent
The Sovereign's Younger Sons

Dukes of England
Dukes of Scotland
Dukes of Great Britain

The Lord Privy Seal
Ambassadors and High Commissioners
The Lord Great Chamberlain
The Lord High Constable
The Earl Marshal
The Lord Steward of the Household
The Lord Chamberlain of the
   Household
The Mast...

Eldest Sons of Dukes
Earls of England TONY.
Earls of Scotland
Earls of Great Britain
Earls of Ireland
Earls of the United Ki...

Royal

CLARENCE HOUSE
S.W.1
5th March 1960

My dearest Sister,

When you and Philip got married, Papa made Philip Duke of Edinburgh on your wedding day. Now that you are the Sovereign, I was thinking that perhaps you could make Tony a Duke on our wedding day – 6th May 1960. We think that DUKE OF BEN NEVIS would be suitable, and as I am your sister I assume he will rank immediately after Philip.

Much love,

Margaret

...ere in existence in Ireland at the ... Great Britain in 1801.
the United Kingdom are those peerages which have been created since 1801.

BUCKINGHAM PALACE

On this the 3rd day of October in the year 1961, Her Majesty Queen Elizabeth the Second has graciously bestowed upon Antony Armstrong-Jones the title first EARL OF SNOWDON.

CLARENCE HOUSE
S.W. 1

6th May 1960

My dear daughter Margaret,

As this is your wedding day, I felt that I must send you a few words, not only to wish you well but to give you some motherly advice. If only your beloved Papa were still with us, I know that he would want to say much the same thing.

If you are to give this marriage a chance, you must stop telling Tony that he resembles Peter Townsend. That is not what a man wants to hear. I know also that you are the daughter of a King of England and have two Queens as your closest relatives, but Margaret, dear, you must not pull rank on your husband, snap your fingers to draw his attention, or insist that he remains standing until you tell him to sit. Think of Kipling, as I do so often, and do not lose the 'common touch'. That is why Lilibet and I are members of the Women's Institute, and why on official engagements I take a snooker cue, or drink a pint of lager, just to show that I can be as common as anyone else. That is why Lilibet keeps racing pigeons and why Philip swears at journalists. As a wedding gift I am giving you a whippet (a downmarket greyhound) which you and Tony can race. Not only is there fun in the sport, but the excellent opportunity to win a few pounds. I know that Tony is not fond of corgis, but trust that he will get to like 'Mother's Ruin', the whippet.

It will be so quiet at Clarence House without you, no 'Chubby Checker' or 'Elvis Presley' echoing from your room, no footmen helping you sneak in through a window at 4.00 a.m. (you thought I didn't know), and no more exciting cocktail parties. When you get to my age it becomes increasingly difficult to accept change. Lilibet has altered the day of Trooping the Colour from Thursday to Saturday, has moved the sentries from the pavement right into the forecourt of Buckingham Palace, and now tells me that we are going to lose the farthing. If Queen Victoria were alive today, she would spin in her grave.

Good luck as you embark on this new life with Tony, and don't worry about me; I shall be very happy here with Ginny, Brandy, Whisky and Sherry, the four corgis.

God Bless.

Love

Mummy

WEDDING PRESENT LIST

Cocktail shaker	Mummy
M̶i̶x̶i̶n̶g̶ ̶	
⋯	⋯
Ice shaver	J̶o̶h̶n̶n̶y̶
Ice tongs	Billy
Lemon slicer	Alice & Henry
Chopping board	Patrick
Gill measure	Peter
Cocktail sticks	Dalrymple-Hamiltons
Cocktail umbrellas	Dominic
Drinking straws	Jocelyn
Decanters for:	Ronald
Gin	
Whisky	Anne
Sherry	Mary
Brandy	Dickie
Port	David & Wallis
Corkscrew	Richard
Bottle opener	Gerald
Cocktail recipe book	George
Small wine glasses ($\frac{3}{4}$ gill)	Jeremy
Ordinary wine glasses (1 gill)	Richard
Cocktail glasses ($\frac{1}{2}$ gill)	Jennifer
Liqueur glasses ($\frac{1}{4}$ gill)	Sharman
Tumblers (2 gills)	Margaret
Pousse-cafe glasses ($\frac{1}{3}$ gill)	Mark
Champagne glasses	Cecil
Brandy glasses (large)	Noël
Soda syphon	Simon
Cigarette lighters (matching pair)	Norman
Cigarette cases (M&A entwined)	John
Plot of land on Mustique	Raine
	Colin

Continued...

From: Morag Auchtermuchty (Mrs)
      Branch Sec. Licensed Victuallers Choir

30th January 1990

Dear Connie,

What a pity Princess Margaret's marriage ended in divorce, because she and Tony would be celebrating their 30th wedding anniversary this year, the 'Pearl', and not only could she have gained a few more necklaces from the Family jewel pool, but you know I always like a good excuse for a knees-up. Angus and I celebrated our 30th in 1988 and what a ceilidh that was. I think everyone enjoyed themselves in the end, although there was a bit of unpleasantness at the start with Angus selling tickets at the door, but I <u>had</u> spent a lot of money on the catering, Connie. I don't know why everyone got upset at having to bring a bottle either; I mean, that's generally accepted now. Even Princess Margaret has it printed on her invitations, and woe betide anyone who forgets.

It was Queen Mary who taught the Royal Family to be thrifty, and you know yourself how the Queen still goes around switching off unnecessary lights. Do you still get twinges in that ankle after your tumble down the Grand Staircase at Buckingham Palace? So much money was spent on bunting, extra champagne glasses and wedding stationery for Princess Margaret's wedding, that it wasn't long before the Duke of Kent got married so that any excesses could be used up. What a charming, unassuming couple they are. I remember once waiting in a crowd to see them, and suddenly I noticed the Duchess standing at my side, among the throng. 'Who are we waiting for?' she asked. I've tried to find some of their correspondence, Connie, but it wasn't easy. They were too shy to write to each other.

Fortunately shyness is not one of Katriona's problems, but sometimes I think she thrusts herself forward too much. Last week I gave Prince Edward a bottle of Glenmuchty whisky to take to Andrew Lloyd Webber to see if he would consider Katriona for 'Aspects of Love', but apparently he's not open to bribery. Angus says that if she married Lloyd Webber she might stand a better chance.

I'll write soon.

Your wee chum,

Morag

Yours, E.

From: Duke of Kent
Dear Hardcastle,

BALMORAL CASTLE

3 August 1958

You omitted to pack my newest suit. Please send it up as soon as possible. Also will you buy me some of the latest neckties. I don't want to look out of place here.

Yours, E.

7 August 1958

From: Duke of Kent
Dear Hardcastle,

BALMORAL CASTLE

Yes, the fishing rod and the clothes arrived safely. The salmon seem to be biting well, but I've had little time for fishing. Would you please oblige by sending up a very large box of chocolates. Soft centres, I think. Please send up my green velvet evening jacket. Get Trumpers to send me some hair oil and some good aftershave.

Yours E.

BALMORAL CASTLE

From: Duke of Kent

Dear Hardcastle,

10 August 1958

      The chocolates were exactly right. Could you get the florists to have a dozen red roses sent up as soon as possible. Haven't seen the River Dee for a week.

               Yours, E.

BALMORAL CASTLE

From: Duke of Kent

12 August 1958

Dear Hardcastle,

      Tomorrow you will receive a trunk back by express containing my best suit, green velvet jacket and various items that I don't need. I am going off alone with my gun to shoot grouse. Don't bother to have any more chocolates or flowers sent up. I was right not to expect there to be anyone decent amongst the house party.

               Yours, E.

Thank you so much for taking me to Kensington Palace last evening to
meet your family. I thoroughly enjoyed myself, but many things surprised me.
Especially when we were having cocktails. You asked for something short, cold
and full of gin, and they fetched Princess Margaret. Everyone was very kind
to me, even though I am not royal. I suspected it was because my father is
Lord Lieutenant of the North Riding of Yorkshire, but Prince Philip seemed
to be more interested in the fact that he was Captain of the Yorkshire County
Cricket Club. I met the Queen briefly, but felt just a little intimidated.
I was so nervous that I blurted out that my family are directly descended from
Oliver Cromwell. 'How charming for you', she smiled and made a hasty retreat.
As Cromwell tried to destroy the monarchy it was perhaps a foolish thing to
have told her. I shall worry about it now.

   Your mother is very beautiful, but I was constantly aware of her watching
me as if weighing me up. She is the Duchess of Kent and what worries me is
that when you and I are married, then I will be Duchess of Kent. It will be
like stealing her title and she'll never like me. That really does worry me.
In fact everyone in the room last night had a title, except me, and even the
dogs were called Prince and Duke. I'm sure that I shall be such an outsider.

               Much love,

                    Katie

Coppins
Iver, Buckinghamshire.

Miss Katharine Worsley   19th July 1960
Hovingham Hall
York, Yorkshire

My darling Katie,

   You do worry far too much. Everyone adored my fiancee, and please
don't be concerned about Mother. She is prepared to revert back to
her old title of Princess Marina just as soon as we're married, so
don't let it bother you any more. I know that you will fit into the
family just perfectly.

   Last night Bysouth, the butler, was ill and I had to get Mother's
maid, Miss Arter, to take over. 'Just stand at the drawing-room door
and call the guests' names as they arrive,' I said. 'Thank you, sir,'
she replied; 'I've been longing to do that for years.'

   Mother and Miss Arter have a love-hate relationship. 'I'll wear
my blue dress this evening, Edith,' Mother will call from the bathroom. 'But she's got a dozen blue dresses,' Miss Arter will grumble.
'How do I know which one she means?'

   We've enrolled her for a series of mind-reading classes now! Do
you have the same problems with your maid?

   I hope that you will be able to come to Balmoral next weekend
as planned. There are so many exciting things to be done there that
I'm sure you will enjoy yourself.

                    Yours,
                        Eddie

Hovingham Hall, York, Yorkshire

Thank you for your reassuring letter, and I shall look forward to visiting Balmoral Castle, but I'm just a little worried because I don't have a lady's maid and I will be travelling up on the night sleeper from York. If it is too embarrassing for me to arrive by taxi, I can always get out at the gates and walk. I would hate to show you up, especially as everyone will be arriving in their Rolls-Royces. I've borrowed some tweeds and a hat for church on Sunday.

As you say, I am sure that there will be lots of exciting things to do and I look forward to it very much.

Love,

Katie

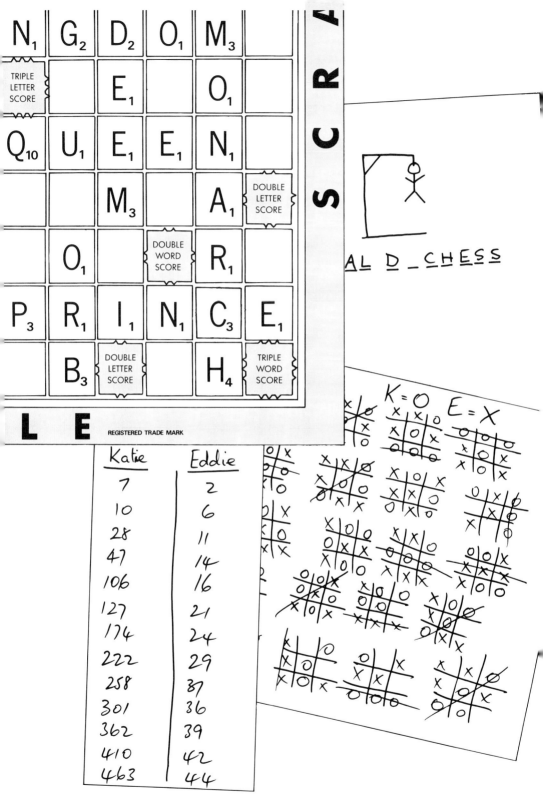

N[1]	G[2]	D[2]	O[1]	M[3]	
TRIPLE LETTER SCORE		E[1]		O[1]	
Q[10]	U[1]	E[1]	E[1]	N[1]	
		M[3]		A[1]	DOUBLE LETTER SCORE
	O[1]		DOUBLE WORD SCORE	R[1]	
P[3]	R[1]	I[1]	N[1]	C[3]	E[1]
	B[3]	DOUBLE LETTER SCORE		H[4]	TRIPLE WORD SCORE

S C R A

L E REGISTERED TRADE MARK

AL D _ CHESS

K = O   E = X

Katie	Eddie
7	2
10	6
28	11
47	14
106	16
127	21
174	24
222	29
258	37
301	36
362	39
410	42
463	44

94

call it), ludo and snakes and ladders, but there is always a
pheasant shoot. So do say you'll come.

You were <u>such</u> a success at Balmoral this summer, sorting out
everyone's worries. It's a shame that Margaret and Tony are having
problems, not speaking to each other, trying to push one another
down the stairs, and so on, but I'm sure these are, as you say, just
teething troubles in their marriage. I know that Margaret appreciated
the time you spent listening to her. Cousin Lilibet is usually more
relaxed, but I do know that this year she was concerned about the
earthquake in Agadir, the United States' Ballistic Missile Early
Warning System at Fylingdales, and the Commons' rejection of the
Wolfenden Committee's recommendations on homosexuality. The end of
British rule in Cyprus on Princess Anne's birthday did not help.
Lilibet hates to see anywhere become a republic.

I look forward to seeing you next week for the full production
of Wagner's Ring Cycle.

Your loving, *Eddie*

95

To Katie,

*Wishing you a Happy Xmas
and a Peaceful New Year*

Margaret.

P.S. Look forward to a
long chat. Tony
is at it again!

Margaret & Tony at Loggerheads.
Austria, 1960.

As you are going to b
sister-in-law, could w
a few words at Christ
I've met a man, but he
years older than me.
will never approve.

Christmas Tree at Coppins.

P.S. I appreciated our talk at
Balmoral. Can we have
another chat at
Christmas? My drinks
so much alcohol, I'm
afraid to let her smoke
in case she ignites.

To the beautiful Katherine

Wishing You a Cool Yule

Love
Tony Armstrong-Jones.

Stormclouds over Kensington Palace. A A-J.

Katie,
    Could you calm my nerves

With D...

Windsor Castle in the snow.

Dear Katie,

A very merry Christmas
and a
Happy New Year

Alexandra

Harry Secombe, Peter Sellers, Michael Bentine
and Spike Milligan sharing a festive beverage.

To Auntie Katie,

Have a ying-tong-ying-tong
celebration!

Love, Charles.

My sister Anne is a pain
in the neck and wants
everything that I want.
But she can't have Wales,
I won't let her.

CRABTREE HALL
CLEGHORN ST PERCY
NORTH YORKSHIRE

1st March 1990

Dear Morag,

Thank you for sending the Kent letters. Once again you managed to underpay the postage. I remember the wedding very well because it took place in York. As minor royals they were not allowed to have St Paul's Cathedral or Westminster Abbey, but the Duchess looked beautiful and has been such an asset to the Royal Family. They telephone her day and night with their problems and she's always happy to sort them out. She even managed to coax Prince Michael down from a tree when he was going through a difficult patch, and offered Prince Edward refuge after he left the Royal Marines and Prince Philip was threatening to shoot him. Of course the Duke and Duchess now have such beautiful, well-adjusted children, and you could do a lot worse than to get your Ewan an introduction to Lady Helen Windsor, or 'Melons' as they call her. I believe your Katriona has a similar nickname, but it escapes me at the moment.

I have managed to obtain a few letters from Princess Alexandra – her daughter Marina has been very happy to let a few family skeletons out of the closet. I thought it best to get these myself as your husband is <u>also</u> called Angus, and it would be most unseemly if his letters to you became muddled up with the Ogilvy correspondence. (I know that your Angus is not the most romantic of men. How anyone can give his wife an oil sump and a carburettor as a birthday present I shall never know.)

I have always been very fond of Princess Alexandra; she is so down to earth. I shall never forget how she visited a hospital in Herefordshire and, referring to the establishment's finances, said to the senior consultant, 'Are you well endowed?' Thank goodness they were close to the powder room and her lady-in-waiting was able to push her quickly inside to save her blushes.

That's all for now. I hope you won't have to go to court over those kilts. I'm sure it must be so easy to muddle the rejects up with the full price stock, especially with Angus's eyesight.

As ever,

Constance

The Dowager Lady Crabtree

98

... ...gus, ever since we met at
the Dorm Beagles Ball eight years ago when you were still a young man, I
have been aware that there is only one person I wish to marry. I was
delighted when you revealed yourself to me at Birkhall this summer and I
knew at last that you feel the same as I. I recently attended the wedding
ceremony of Princess Sophie to Prince Juan Carlos of Spain, and although
every eligible European Prince seemed to have his attention pushed upon me
by a domineering European Mother, I know that you are the only man for me.

Although I have reached an age at which I don't have to seek the
Queen's permission to marry, I am only too aware of the obstacles that
royalty face when marrying commoners. Look at my cousin Margaret. She
arrived recently to inspect a guard of honour wearing a mini-skirt and a
Mickey Mouse watch on her wrist. Already she seems to be more common than
royal. Could the same happen to me? I know that when I was studying
nursing, I once went on a bus and actually enjoyed it. Mother would never
forgive me if I became too ordinary. At home we still have to dress for
breakfast, and always have silver-plated cereal bowls, and croissants
brought to us hot from Fortnum and Mason, even when we are at Coppins in
the country. A whole train comes each day to Iver station with our bread
delivery. That, says Mother, is what being royal is all about. When
Marilyn Monroe telephoned the other day to invite my mother to a film
premiere she was told that 'Princess Marina has never heard of you.' That
is style. When we have a room decorated Mother dabs a little of her face
powder on the wall and that is then the colour in which the room is
decorated, so that our house matches her complexion. (A little tip she was
given by Wallis Simpson.) Mother also has her hair washed six times every
day. I'm not sure that I would be able to maintain such high standards.
If Mother ever found out that you and I had once eaten in a transport cafe
I think I would be disinherited.

love
Alexandra

From: The Hon. Angus Ogilvy

Cortachy Castle,
Kirriemuir,
Angus,
Scotland.

20th November 1962

My dear Alexandra,

I do appreciate your concerns about my non-royal birth, but I am sure that we can bring your family round. After all, unlike the Snowdons, my family have their own castle. My father is an earl and was lord-in-waiting to King George V, and Lord Chamberlain to the Queen Mother. And my mother, Mabell, was a lady-in-waiting and confidante to your grandmother for nearly fifty years, so I think this places the Ogilvies at least on the steps of the throne, if not anywhere near the seat. If all that fails, you can always promise them some grouse from our estate - that should swing it. Either way, if a photographer can marry the Queen's only sister, I'm sure that a successful businessman such as myself should be acceptable. I have widespread business interests and a very substantial shareholding in a Rhodesian company called Lonrho, so can at least keep you in the style to which you have become accustomed. It may not be bread from Fortnum's, but it can be haggis and oatcakes from Forfar. Plus Arbroath smokies to your heart's content. So please, let's approach your mother this week. Let us marry while I'm still of an age to walk down the aisle without sticks.

Truly yours,

Angus

KENSINGTON PALACE

* * *   29th November 1962   * * *   5.15 p.m.   * * *

It is with the greatest pleasure that Princess Marina, Duchess of Kent, announces the betrothal of her daughter Princess Alexandra to Mr Angus Ogilvy, second son of the Earl and Countess of Airlie, to which union The Queen has gladly given her consent.

I must admit that I had my reservations about Angus at first. As you know, the Kent family have never had a great deal of money, and I have to sell a Fabergé egg most years to buy new outfits, so I did hope that you would marry someone rich. Nevertheless, I hope that I have been able to help you so far with the Valenciennes lace which belonged to my mother, and a veil worn by Princess Patricia of Connaught, which should have saved money on your wedding dress. I know that some members of the family frowned at the idea of placing a 'wants' list with Harrods, but it does avoid the duplication of wedding presents and I am sure that the idea will catch on with other members of the Family. The British always wait for a European to take the initiative. The Queen Mother would never have thought of Powder Blue if I hadn't introduced Marina Blue, and look how the British fashion industry received a boost when I began wearing pillbox hats.

In your married life I would suggest that you accept as many luncheon and dinner engagements as possible, as that will drastically reduce your food bills, and make sure that Angus has a good business lunch. Try and get the Queen to give Angus a title, as she did for Tony Armstrong-Jones, as that will increase his business standing and will result in the offer of more directorships. I know that you have never worried too much about clothes, but from now onwards you must not choose anything youthful, but stick to classic suits so that the age difference between yourself and Angus does not appear so great. I am sending you one of Queen Mary's walking sticks, which might help. It's certainly worked for the Queen; no one would ever realise that Prince Philip is seven years older (we Greeks have good bone structure, you see).

How thoughtful of Angus to give you a tiara as a wedding gift, and I notice that the pearls unscrew so that turquoises can be inserted for informal occasions. How very practical and economic. Two for the price of one. Angus is obviously very proud of his Scottish ancestry. Only last week he asked me the difference between a Scotsman and a canoe. (The canoe tips.) I notice that he wears a modern wristwatch. He obviously hates taking anything out of his pocket.

I gather that the Queen Mother is lending you Birkhall for the honeymoon. How kind. That will certainly save money. Of course, she is a Scot, too. 'Granny Glamis', her staff call her.

Have a happy wedding day and a long and happy married life.

All my love,
Mother.

P.S. If you get Snowdon instead of Beaton to take the wedding photos it will be much cheaper. Keep it in the family.

Dinner service | Cutlery
Glasses | Ornaments
Crockery | Tablecloth
Car | Napkins
Chauffeur | Light bulbs
Housemaid | Furniture polish
Cook | Wardrobes
Butler | Garage
Valet | Dinner gong
Dresser | Mirrors

FOOD REQUIRED FOR WEDDING BREAKFAST

80 lb smoked salmon
500 oz caviar
200 chickens
50 ducks
36 turkeys
2 barons of beef
14 legs of pork
24 hams

DRINK FOR WEDDING BREAKFAST

1,600 bottles of champagne
15 dozen cases of whisky
10 cases of gin
3 cases of vodka
2,000 bottles of beer

Couldn't we ask people to bring sandwiches?

A

That's Princess Margaret sorted out, what about the rest of us?

A

ITINERARY

Wednesday 24th April 1963

Where do I fit in? A

10.30   The Queen and Prince Philip will leave Windsor Castle.
11.00   Non-royal guests will arrive at Westminster Abbey.
11.15   Bridegroom will leave Culross Street, arrive 11.30,
        Cloisters Door.
11.20   The Bridesmaid's motorcade procession will leave Buckingham
        Palace, arrive 11.30, West Door.
11.30   Princess Marina will leave Buckingham Palace, arrive 11.45,
        West Door.
11.37   Princess Margaret will leave Buckingham Palace, arrive 11.52,
        West Door.
11.38   Lord Snowdon will leave Kensington Palace, arrive 11.53,

WEDDING CAKE

6 lb butter
6 lb sugar
70 eggs
12½ lb currants
7 lb flour
46 lb marzipan
25 lb Royal icing
spices
2 bottles rum
2 bottles brandy

Decorate with roses for Alexandra
and bagpipes with tartan windbag
for Angus.

Might it not be better to have a sponge? A!

second w[...] [...]oking around the stables) found a few [...]
Anyway, poking around the stables) found a few [...]
that had been ripped apart, but)'ve managed to
piece them together. Poor Mark is living in a barn
with just an oil stove and a tilly lamp with
scarcely a horseshoe to call his own.) think work
has been to blame. They'd been separated six months
before he realised. When Anne failed to turn up
for one of their twice-yearly meetings he knew
something must be wrong.) suppose that once they'd
both stopped competing in three-day events there
was nothing left to talk about.

Of course,) knew the marriage was over when she
accepted the title of Princess Royal, which meant
she didn't have to call herself Mrs Mark
Phillips any more.)'ve got a nose for these kind
of things.)'ve told Mark that once they are
finally divorced he is welcome to come up to
Scotland and meet Katriona any time.

Your wee chum,
Morag

P.s.) enclose my hotel and travel expenses.

BUCKINGHAM PALACE

31st May 1971

Lieutenant Mark Phillips,
1st The Queen's Dragoon Guards,
Sandhurst, Berkshire.

Dear Lieutenant Phillips,

One would very much like to say that one was very pleased to see one win the one major prize at this year's Badminton Horse Trials. So one wanted to say congratulations on coming first. One did not do as well as one would have liked oneself, but being one's first international competition one was wondrous at coming in fifth.

One hopes to meet one at the European Championships in Burghley in September.

Yours sincerely,

Anne

Royal Highness The Princess Anne.

1st THE QUEEN'S DRAGOON GUARDS

Sandhurst, Berkshire.
2nd June 1971

Dear Princess Anne,

Thank you for your letter. I hadn't realised that you had taken part in the competition until I received it. I look forward to having a jump off against the clock with you at Burghley and maybe we might have a dance together at the Hunt Ball.

Yours sincerely,
Mark Phillips

BUCKINGHAM PALACE

4th June 1971

Dear Lieutenant Phillips,

One would very much like to dance with one, but does one have any royal connections? When one's mother is Queen, one cannot dance with just anyone.

Yours sincerely,

Anne

Her Royal Highness The Princess Anne.

_____, who married the seventh Earl of Cardigan who led the Charge of the Light Brigade. Perhaps that is where I get my love of equestrian sports. Do you have any famous ancestors? Are your family interested in horses? Indeed, who are your family?

Yours,

Mark

8th June 1971

Dear Mark,

   Is one thick or something? You know when one licks a stamp to put on a letter? Well, one is then licking my mother on the back of the head. We are the Royal Family. By that I don't mean the royal 'we', which Mother can use when she means 'one', but one's family as a whole.

   Gan-Gan, that was one's great-grandmother Queen Mary, used to tell an amusing story about the royal 'we'. She once went to a London theatre where there was no royal loo in the royal box. The management had put out a commode for her use, not knowing that she never used anyone else's facilities anyway. The following morning the manager did his rounds, and finding the royal receptacle empty, he decided to use it himself. Later that morning as the cleaning ladies left, they waved little bottles at him. 'We may not have seen the Queen, but we've got something of hers to remember her by!' There are probably still little bottles around labelled 'Royal Wee'. One often laughs to oneself over this when one's burdens feel onerous, as one can imagine.

   If one's horse 'Doublet' is fit, one will be taking part in the European Championships this year.

Yours sincerely,

Anne

MOUNT HOUSE
Great Somerford
Wiltshire

16th August, 1971

Dear Princess Anne,

I was very concerned to read in the newspapers today that you had collapsed with severe stomach pains. At first I thought it must have been something you had eaten on your birthday, but we are told that it is an ovarian cyst. What bad luck, with the European Championships barely two weeks away. Obviously you will not be riding for some time, but if you would like to come to my parents' home in Wiltshire to convalesce, you could at least watch me compete on the television. Unlike your family, we have a colour set. Get well soon,

Yours,

Mark

St Mary's Hospital

... ... be turning pro in the European Championships
and shall be back in the saddle well in time for the first
day on 2nd September. Good lord, man, that's over ten days
away. One isn't going to lie in bed all day just
because one has had surgery. One must keep occupied.
I've taken the opportunity officially to open ten wards here,
as well as unveil a plaque on a new kidney dialysis
machine, present prizes to the first child to use a bedpan
in the children's ward today, and persuade a senior
surgeon to make a considerable donation to Save the
Children. We did mention Knighthoods, but at no time
did one say that one could get him one. If he
misunderstood my words then that's his fault, not mine.
One's Gan-Gan taught one here to be idle. 'Incapacitated'
was not a word in her vocabulary.

Be prepared to do battle
at the European Championships!

Anne

BUCKINGHAM PALACE

6th September 1971

Dear Mark,

Well, one won! It was a bit hairy on the final day with twelve fences still to jump. I knew that I had to clear ten to win the Championship, but what a surprise to clear all twelve and to find oneself World Champion, too. Mummy was so excited when she presented me with the trophy and medal that it was as much as she could do to stop herself jumping up and down. Jolly bad luck that you didn't make it on 'Great Ovation', but I look forward to doing even greater battles with you in the future.

Yours,

Anne

... ... London flowers, excited when you were
given the Sportswriters' Award, and overcome when those storytellers
at Fleet Street made you National Press Sportswoman of 1971. But
Anne, dear, as your mother and Queen I feel that I must warn you
against becoming big-headed over this. I know that you are being
feted and praised from every direction, but there is such a danger
in this. Look at your Auntie Margaret. Once she could do no wrong
in the eyes of the press, and now she can do nothing right. There
is such a temptation to place royalty on a pedestal, but once up
there I must say that there is an even greater temptation to knock
us down. That is why your father never panders to the press; having
been in the Navy, he likes to keep things on an even keel.

Now that you are famous, men will be throwing themselves at you,
and although you may be tempted by Richard Meade, you know only too
well from the scenes we have every summer at Balmoral when Auntie
Margaret and Uncle Tony come to stay, that marrying a commoner can
only spell disaster in the end.

Finally, Anne, I don't want to cause offence, and I can understand
that you needed new stationery printed now that you are undertaking
royal duties, but don't you think your choice is just a little
unsubtle?

            Your ever loving   *Mummy*

P.S. Don't forget Charles' birthday tomorrow.

111

BUCKINGHAM PALACE

From: Her Royal Highness THE Princess Anne
WORLD CHAMPION

14th November 1971

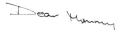

Naff off! This notepaper cost half my Civil List allowance and I happen to like it.

I know that you are very concerned about the man I eventually marry, and that you think I should marry someone royal, but come off it, Mum, I'm 21 now and you're not Queen Victoria. I'm not a pawn in the game of Europe where I have to marry someone in Lithuania or the Falklands. This is 1971, nobody's going to invade us or declare war against us. I want to marry for love, not for a national defence policy. Marrying a commoner is no bad thing and I am certain that Auntie Margaret and Uncle Tony are happy really. Throwing things at each other and screaming at the tops of their voices is really just a ritual, a way of showing affection. When the Sèvres vase hit

keep Father happy. His father is a landowner and a major in the King's
Dragoon Guards, and Mark is himself in your Dragoon Guards, so that should
keep you happy. He had his first pony when he was three and knows very little
about anything except horses, so that keeps me happy.

Can he come to Sandringham at New Year to meet you?

> Your loving daughter who will do anything for
> her country and work every hour God sends, just
> as long as you say 'yes',
>
> Anne

SANDRINGHAM HOUSE

1st December 1971

My dear Anne,

Sorry I have not replied to your letter sooner, but I am still trying to work this decimal coinage out. As I never use money it makes no sense to me whatsoever. As my head is on the money you'd think the least this Government could do would be to ask my opinion first. I think it is Edward Heath's way of pushing us into Europe. It would be too much to make us join overnight, so I think he's doing it bit by bit. If I'm not careful it will be weights and measures next (I will warn him that I am the <u>ruler</u> and I want to keep twelve inches to the foot, not ten), then we'll be joining the Common Market. Before you know it, everyone will be speaking Esperanto and I'll be pensioned off altogether. Don't let Europe Rule Britannia, your father says.

No, Anne, I don't think this Mark can come to Sandringham at New Year. You know how the press hide in bushes. One sighting of you together and they'll have you married off. Anyway, I know nothing about him. I didn't know there was a Prince Mark. Which country is he from? Is he in league with Edward Heath? A European infiltrated into our midst could spell the end of the monarchy.

Whatever happens, Anne, you know that you will not be able to marry next year. Your father and I celebrate our Silver Wedding Anniversary in 1972, and we cannot possibly have a wedding spoiling the national celebrations. Besides, I'm having special five-shilling pieces (crowns),

P.S. If you are to see this Mark again, find out
    a) Is he English, or from the Commonwealth at least?
    b) Is he much older than you?
    c) Has he ever been divorced?
    d) Does he know the third verse of the National Anthem? (It's so
embarrassing when people don't.)
    e) Has he ever been interviewed by Simon Dee?
    f) Are there any haemophiliacs in his family?

These questions could be crucial to his future...

BUCKINGHAM PALACE

23 November 1972

Dear Mummy and Daddy,

        I hope that you have both recovered from your wedding
anniversary celebrations and can now relax with Uncle Harold and
Auntie Zia at Luton Hoo. As much as Mark and one would like to
have got married this year, one does see that you were right. So
much preparation was involved in getting Westminster Abbey ready
for your Thanksgiving Service that a wedding would have been out of
the question. If only the Duke of Gloucester could have waited a
little while longer before marrying Birgitte van Deurs, they
wouldn't have been forced to have the ceremony at St Andrew's
Church, Barnwell, with scarcely a photographer, let alone a
television camera in sight.
        I think that Mark must be going to ask me to be his wife
because the other day we were looking at riding hats and he said
that I look much better in the £45.00 one than the £72.00 one.
Only a prospective husband can say that. I know he isn't royal,
Mummy, but he is a Phillips and I know that you have always been
happy with Philips.
        Must dash. I'm planning a weekend trip to Somalia.

                    Love, Anne

115

MOUNT HOUSE
Great Somerford
Wiltshire

5th April 1973

My dear Anne,

Last night I asked your father if I could marry you. 'Can you support a family?' he asked.

'No, sir, I was only planning to support your daughter. I thought the rest of you had the Civil List,' I said.

He looked a bit puzzled, so I tried again.

'Sir, if I may, I would like to have your daughter's hand in marriage.'

'Sorry, that's, er, not possible,' he grinned. (I thought for a moment I was unsuitable, but honestly I've never been divorced.) 'If you marry her hand, you'll have to have the rest of her as well.'

So he has agreed, and your mother is having a vellum document of consent drawn up. Your father is very nice, but he does have a strange sense of humour. He kept saying things like, 'Have the marriage ceremony in the morning, then if it doesn't work out you won't have wasted the whole day.' Then he said, 'When my sister-in-law Margaret got married, it wasn't by the Archbishop of Canterbury but by the Minister of War.' I didn't know that. I was only about twelve when they got married, but I could have sworn it was the Archbishop of Canterbury.

I heard today that I am being promoted to a Captain of the Queen's Dragoon Guards. Now the Queen's daughter will not have to marry a Lieutenant. I am very excited. As I am Mark Anthony, do say that you will be my Cleopatra so that we can gallop down the Nile together.

All my love,

Mark

The Gambia
10/4/73

POST   CARD

 ...be as much a commoner as possible. Don't _ever_ accept
another title from them, or they'll have you an Earl
before you can say Princess Royal. I'm not having any
kids of ours growing up with the millstone of a title
around their necks. Look what happened to Auntie
Margaret as soon as they made Tony an Earl. In future
any kind of promotion for you is out. Got it,
dunderhead?

 Love you,

Anne

BUCKINGHAM PALACE

* * *   30th May 1973   * * *   11.00 a.m.   * * *

It is with the greatest pleasure that The Queen and The Duke
of Edinburgh announce the betrothal of their beloved daughter
The Princess Anne to Captain Mark Phillips, The Queen's Dragoon
Guards, son of Major and Mrs Peter Phillips.

BUCKINGHAM PALACE

13 November 1973.

My dear Anne,

It seems impossible for me to believe that my own little daughter will be following in my footsteps and walking down the aisle at Westminster Abbey as a bride. If they haven't hammered it in, watch out for a nail near the altar. I caught my train on it on the way into the vestry to sign the register. It was very thoughtful of you to have the ceremony on Charles's birthday, it does save us having to have two cakes and I know you won't mind a few candles on the bottom tier just to please him.

At this time it is a mother's duty to prepare her daughter for her wedding night. When I got married Granny told me to lie back and think of the Commonwealth, but I think you'll have your work cut out showing Mark what to do. I've asked the Apothecary to the Household to prescribe a few herbal pills just to calm him down, and I enclose a copy of something Auntie Margaret suggests. Be gentle with him, Anne, and don't frighten him as you might put him off for life and at the moment you are my only hope of grandchildren. Charles has been married off so many times by the press, but looks to be no nearer to finding a bride. Andrew and Edward are still far too young to think about girls, so my hopes lie with you. With any luck Mark will have picked up a few tips in the Dragoons, but don't let him do anything with his busby, and please don't wear your Zandra Rhodes nightie, that could only make matters worse.

Already your father and I are thinking up titles for Mark. It makes a change from playing Scrabble, and we hope to let you know what we have chosen soon. When you do have children we don't want them to be born commoners, do we? I hope you will accept the title as my gift.

Your ever loving,

Why Can't I have a toaster like any other bride? Anne

Mummy

P.S. If there are any problems there is always a bed for you here.

3 dashes of lime juice
3/4 gill of Famous Grouse whisky
1 dash of sugar syrup

Garnish with a slice of lime, sprig of mint and
a piece of sugar cane.

Stir and serve with ice. Drink the cocktail in one go and
then head straight for the bedroom.

After our wedding night Tony said he felt like a new man.
I did too.

Weave a circle round him thrice,
And close your eyes with holy dread
For he on honeydew hath fed
And drunk the milk of Paradise.

S.T. Coleridge

In the morning you might need one of my hangover cures:

Suffering Bastard

1/2 jigger of brandy
1/2 jigger of gin
1/2 jigger of lime juice
2 dashes of bitters

Mix, drink and smile.

Hair of the Corgi

Large measure of whisky
1 tablespoon of honey
1 tablespoon of cream

I find this makes an
excellent breakfast most
mornings.

BUCKINGHAM PALACE

16 January 1961.

Dear Philip,

I think it is about time you told Charles the facts of life.
Anne is very mature, so you might as well tell her at the same time,
but Andrew is too young to know.

1/ Tell them that Little Princes are different from Little
Princesses. The former wear uniforms, the latter tiaras.

2/ Use dogs as an example, rather than the birds and bees. If two
corgis rub noses, they have a little puppy. Tell them not to
touch other people's dogs - they might get bitten.

3/ Tell them royal hands are for waving and must be kept out of
the bedclothes at night in case someone comes into the room.

4/ Warn Charles about boys at school who get over-friendly.

Don't use any Navy terms, we don't want to frighten Charles.
The future of the monarchy is in his hands.

Lilibet

try to get him in the showers. He is not to undress in front of anyone at any time.

3/ Tell Sarah never to have her photograph taken in Pimlico. Look what happened to me. She is not to go into a darkroom to see if anything will develop.

4/ Show them some tasteful photographs to explain the differences between men and women. A picture says a thousand words. No close-ups, though.

Margaret

16th May 1989

Dear Mark,

Peter will be twelve this year and boys develop fast, so I think you should tell him the facts of life. As we won't be a family by next year, you might as well tell Zara as well. Girls develop even faster.

These are the main points to explain:

1/ Foreplay
2/ Masturbation
3/ Intercourse
4/ Different forms of contraception
5/ Homosexuality
6/ AIDS (demonstrate a condom)
7/ The G-spot
8/ Orgasm
9/ Pregnancy
10/ Hormones
11/ The menopause
12/ Menstruation

Anne.

From: Morag Auchtermuchty (Mrs)
      President Licensed Victuallers Choir

31st August 1990

Dear Connie,

    Well, this is the first anniversary of Anne and Mark's separation.
Thank goodness Buckingham Palace kept the wording of the Snowdon separation
announcement on the word processor (the one Ronnie Reagan gave the Queen),
as that saved a lot of time. How odd that both Princess Anne's and
Princess Margaret's marriages should last exactly sixteen years. It's
probably something in their hormones. Of course, there's much speculation
now about Princess Anne and the equerry, Timothy Lawrence. Doesn't he look
so much like the other equerry, Peter Townsend? They could almost be
brothers. Princess Margaret has decided not to remarry, to avoid the
age-old royal problem of a divorcee marrying in church, but what will
happen when Anne wants to remarry? Thank goodness Wallis Simpson isn't
alive to see it. There would have been ructions there, Connie, I can tell
you.

    What a fuss there was a while back when some of Timothy Lawrence's
letters to Princess Anne were stolen. The newspapers got a lot of mileage
out of that, but as you and I know, they weren't love letters at all.
Otherwise the press would have published and been damned. So innocuous was
the correspondence that it created a much better scandal to hand it over to
Scotland Yard, promising not to reveal a word of the contents. The
public's imagination invented a story far more exciting than any Barbara
Cartland novel.

    Although nothing to do with love, I think you should take a gamble and
print the letters from Timbo so that the world can at last see what all the
fuss was about.

                        Your wee chum,

                        Morag

P.S. That new ointment has worked wonders on Katriona's spots. Admittedly
      it took off a layer of skin, but then she has plenty to spare.

122

Equerry's Office, Buckingham Palace   6 February '89

To The Princess Royal

Your Royal Highness,
     [blurred text] ... British Knitting & Clothing Export Council.

Commander Timothy Lawrence

Equerry's Office, Buckingham Palace   6 February '89

To The Princess Royal

Your Royal Highness,
     I must apologise for not bringing the umbrella today. I know it once
belonged to Queen Mary and is of sentimental value. It was my fault entirely.
I will bring it tomorrow on your visit to the Royal Naval Museum, Portsmouth.

     Commander Timothy Lawrence

Equerry's Office, Buckingham Palace   8 February '89

To The Princess Royal

Your Royal Highness,
     At last you have been reunited with your umbrella and I'm glad that it
came in useful on your visit to Portsmouth. Hampshire is my home county and
it is so often wet there. It is due to rain all week so I would advise, Ma'am,
that you bring it on your visit to the Detention Centre for Young Offenders
tomorrow.

Commander Timothy Lawrence

Equerry's Office, Buckingham Palace   10 February '89

To The Princess Royal

Your Royal Highness,
     I was most distressed that your umbrella was stolen yesterday.
I trust that Scotland Yard will look into the matter.

Commander Timothy Lawrence

How fortunate Commander Lawrence kept carbon copies. Morag

I do like your idea of setting up a commune, although I'm not sure that I could come and live on it as you suggest, MUCH as I would like to sometimes! I am still married to Tony in name and I've caused my sister enough headaches. I did enjoy disguising myself as your mother to look at suitable properties. Although Bayham Abbey was nice and I do like Kent, I couldn't possibly have let you live there, which was the reason for my fainting fit and sudden migraine. Do you know who that woman was who opened the door to us? The former Mrs Peter Townsend! How could I possibly have visited you there? No, I think Surrendell Farm will suit you fine, and it's not too far from my friends the Frys, so I can visit whenever I stay with them.

I enclose your ticket to Mustique and I will meet you in Basil's Bar as arranged. If anyone asks you who you are, just tell them that you're Lord Snowdon and you've had a face-lift. You do look like a younger version of him anyway, although you are at least an inch bigger, but I don't expect anyone will notice.

I cannot wait to get away to the sun. Lilibet's given me some boring engagements this season. Last night we had an aged actress here to dinner. Not so much a has-been as a never-was.

'I couldn't think of doing anything else,' she said, 'I'm wedded to the theatre.'

'Then why don't you sue it for non-support?' I asked. She was not amused. Socially she really is the creme-de-la-crumb, but she does a lot for charity and is hankering after a damehood, so yours truly is left to entertain.

Tony is now in Australia working on a new film. Once again he's taken Lucy Lindsay-Hogg, his production assistant. He takes her on every assignment. People will begin to talk. How dare he leave me here on my own. Must close as I'm off to a cocktail party, then off to Covent Garden to see 'Manon' for the umpteenth time, but it's one of my favourites. See you on Mustique. Don't forget your Bermuda shorts! Oh, and don't forget your full allowance of duty-frees.

Love, Margaret.

KENSINGTON PALACE

Apartment 1A
Clock Court
19th March, 1976.

Dear Roddy,

At last Lilibet has agreed that Tony and I can publicly part. It's taken ten years and a lot of red tape to get through the Royal Separation Act of 1536, especially as I didn't want to have my head chopped off. (they really should bring those clauses into the twentieth century). The separation is amicable and we've agreed to split the house fifty-fifty. He has the outside, I have the inside. I'm turning his study into a little cocktail bar, and think I'll keep his darkroom as it is. You could always quit the commune and move into Tony's toolshed if it would make life any easier for you.

I am going officially to Morocco and Tunisia next month. Lilibet always gets prickly heat in the sun so she's going to Bradford and Sunderland, so you can come as part of my luggage if you wish. We'll have to disguise you as a trunky just in case it looks as if I'm smuggling Tony out of the country.

Love, Margaret.

KENSINGTON PALACE

* * * 19th March 1976 * * * 4.00 p.m. * * *

Her Royal Highness The Princess Margaret, Countess of Snowdon, and the Earl of Snowdon have mutually agreed to live apart. The Princess will carry out her public duties and functions unaccompanied by Lord Snowdon. There are no plans for divorce proceedings.

Surrendell Farm
(Potting shed)
Wiltshire.

~... Margaret old fruit, ... my Ian Claude

Roddy. xx

POST   CARD

30th November, 1978.

Dear Lilibet,

Enjoying the sun on
this official visit. Tired,
but happy. Tony and I
are still friends and I
know that Roddy loves me.
Now I have the best of
both worlds.

Margo.

Lifeguard, Fiji.

Her Majesty Queen Elizabeth II

Buckingham Palace

London SW1A 1BR

_____

_____

127

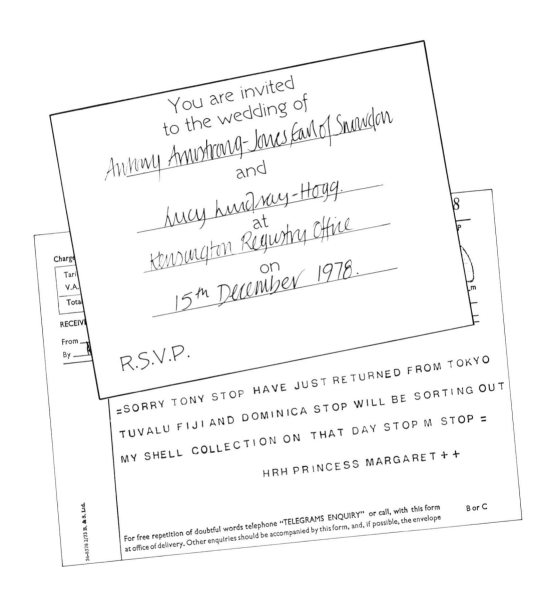

You are invited
to the wedding of
Anthony Armstrong-Jones, Earl of Snowdon
and

Lucy Lindsay-Hogg.
at
Kensington Registry Office
on
15th December 1978.

R.S.V.P.

=SORRY TONY STOP HAVE JUST RETURNED FROM TOKYO

TUVALU FIJI AND DOMINICA STOP WILL BE SORTING OUT

MY SHELL COLLECTION ON THAT DAY STOP M STOP =

HRH PRINCESS MARGARET + +

Charge

Tari
V.A.
Total

RECEIV

From
By

For free repetition of doubtful words telephone "TELEGRAMS ENQUIRY" or call, with this form
at office of delivery. Other enquiries should be accompanied by this form, and, if possible, the envelope

B or C

5e-8578 2/73 B. & S. Ltd.

Roderick Llewelyn

and

Marlow, Bucks.

R.S.V.P.

6th July 1981 — Princess Margaret left Heathrow Airport this morning for a fifteen-day official visit to Canada.

POST   CARD

Toronto   11 July · 1981.

Dear Lilibet,
Am thoroughly fed up. I'm all alone now. Divorced, old and unloved. May not return from Canada.
        Margo.

Queen Elizabeth II.

Buckingham Palace,

London SW1A 1BR.

129

AUCHTERMUCHTY WHISKY DISTILLERY
WOOLLEN MILL & CAR REPAIR SERVICE
PERTHSHIRE, SCOTLAND

From: Morag Auchtermuchty (Mrs)
        Ex-President Licensed Victuallers Choir

1st September 1990

Dear Connie,

    What sad love-lives Princess Margaret and the Princess Royal have had.
Fortunately they have not allowed things to get them down, and both are
still celebrating the Queen Mother's 90th birthday. What a celebration
that was. Dancing on the table, swinging from the chandeliers, running
naked through the heather. I know I should have controlled myself, but you
know what I'm like when I've had one malt too many, Connie. All the Royal
Family have been up to Balmoral this year, except Prince and Princess
Michael of Kent, of course. Not surprisingly, I think the Queen feels a
wee bit intimidated by Princess Michael, who has such high standards.
Princess Michael's a stickler for etiquette, and the Queen just wants to
relax when she gets up here. You can understand it, Connie, you don't want
the National Anthem every time you walk into a room or long speeches after
every meal when you're on holiday. They get enough of that the rest of the
year.
    The poor Queen seems to be dogged by the Royal Marriages Act, and
Princess Michael contravened every clause. Not only was she divorced, but
to cap it all she was a Roman Catholic. Even Wallis Simpson was Church of
England. Like a latter-day Edward VIII, Prince Michael had to renounce his
rights of succession to marry her. The path of true love, Connie.

Your wee chum,

Morag

21st April 1978

Dearest Marie-Christine,

Now that your marriage to Tom Troubridge has been officially
annulled by the Roman Catholic Church, I wondered if we might
tell my cousin Lilibet that we wish to marry. As Princess
Margaret's divorce comes through this year, I am certain that
my cousin will be thrilled by some good news at last.

All my love,

Michael

1 Grand Manor,
Chelsea,
London SW3.

22nd April 1978

By all means tell the Queen about us. (Why wasn't I included in the guest list for her birthday party yesterday? 900 years of breeding in my family must count for something.) While you're at it, tell her that I don't want St Paul's Cathedral. I don't see why we cannot use the Coronation State coach either. It was used for the Jubilee last year so we know it still moves. What's the point of shutting it away until the next Coronation? That could be the next century. Tell your cousin Lilibet that I will be happy to recommend my dress designer to her if she wants it. Oh, and tell her she shouldn't wear brown. It does nothing for her skin.

Hopefully there will be a grace-and-favour residence going. After all, I will be a Princess when we're married. I think the Tower of London would suit me fine. Nicht wa?

Yours sincerely,

BARONESS MARIE-CHRISTINE VON REIBNITZ

23rd April 1978

Dear Marie-Christine,

I visited my cousin at Windsor last night. Unfortunately she was not as excited about our wedding plans as I would have hoped. She gasped 'Divorce' and clutched at her three rows of pearls, and we spent the rest of the evening picking pearls up from the floor of her private sitting-room. Certainly it was not the time to tell her that you are also Roman Catholic. I'm sorry, MC, but it's not going to be quite such plain sailing as I had hoped.

I had a quiet word with Princess Margaret today, who is an expert on these matters, and she said that I might have to give up my rights of succession if I were to marry a Roman Catholic. It's a bit of a fix, I know, but I'm sure we will be able to sort something out.

All my love,

Michael

1 Grand Manor,
Chelsea,
London SW3.

24th April 1978

Polish Count. That must ████ ███ ████ for something.

Yours sincerely,

BARONESS MARIE-CHRISTINE VON REIBNITZ

THE ROYAL HUSSARS

Darling Marie-Christine,

25th April 1978

You didn't tell me that your mother had been divorced as well. Cousin Lilibet really never would stand for that. It must be kept quiet at all costs. Princess Margaret tells me that she has discovered we cannot marry in church because of your divorce, and I cannot marry in a registry office because I am royal, so we can only marry abroad, but you must agree that any children we have will be brought up in the Anglican faith, Lilibet being Head of the Church, Defender of the Faith and all that.

All my love,

Michael

1 Grand Manor,
Chelsea,
London SW3.

26th April 1978

Dear Prince Michael,

How familiar of you to call me 'darling' when you don't even know if we can marry yet. That Princess Margaret is probably only telling you those things. Jealous because she's lost her own husband. Jealous because I'm twice her height. (Her drawing-room curtains don't go with the carpet, so she's probably colour blind anyway.) How can I, a good Catholic girl, have Anglican children? I would feel a failure as a mother. Perhaps at least the English would then like me, though you British hate anyone who's a success. See if your cousin will let us be King and Queen of America. They hate failure there.

Yours sincerely,

BARONESS MARIE-CHRISTINE VON REIBNITZ

28th April 1978

My Marie-Christine,

Sorry, but your suggestions really will not wash with Lilibet. She's had too much experience of life to be bamboozled into things. As you feel so strongly about your religion and your position, perhaps you are marrying the wrong man. Why not introduce yourself to Prince Charles? He's eligible and has good prospects. Sorry if I'm not good enough for you.

Goodbye,

Michael of Kent

1 Grand Manor,
Chelsea,
London SW3

. . . engagements. Even the occasional
luncheon. Ask your cousin about a Civil List allowance for us.

I love you,

Marie-Christine

KENSINGTON PALACE

1st May 1978

My darling Marie-Christine,

You've made me a very happy man. As you love me I know that you will
marry me regardless of my income or position. Because you love me, I know,
I have no fear in telling you that you could not ever be Princess
Marie-Christine as you are not royal in your own right. You will have to
take my name and be known as Princess Michael.

All my love,

Michael

1 Grand Manor,
Chelsea,
London SW3.

2nd May 1978

Michael,

How dare you 'My darling' me. What do you mean, 'not royal in my own right'? I'm more royal than the whole lot of your family put together. Who does your cousin think she is — Mrs High and Mighty — insisting I be called Princess Michael. With my height people will think I'm a female impersonator. To your narrow-minded family, 'abroad' is anywhere outside the Palace gates!

Well, if I am to comply with your silly English customs and be saddled with the name Princess Michael, I shall make certain it is a name that is known. Not like your sister, Alexandra, who can shop in Safeway's unrecognised. If the Queen will not give us a Civil List income then I shall simply have to make some money myself. I shall continue with my own interior design company, Szapar Designs, and you can get me a commission to redesign Buckingham Palace. It's like a museum with not a Fortuny fabric in sight, and it can't have had a lick of paint since Queen Victoria's time. And look at Clarence House! All that chintz, it's like sitting in the Chelsea Flower Show. I shall also write books about 'Royal Outsiders' and shall visit her Royal Highness the Duchess of Windsor for help.

At all times, Michael, we shall prove that we are not second-class royals. I will wear a tiara whenever I am in public, we <u>must</u> have a home with a balcony to wave from, and I shall contact the Post Office to see if my face can be put on a stamp. The peasants must be sick of seeing Lilibet's face on their letters for more than twenty-five years.

Please find enclosed

Does your brother _really_ need the title 'Duke of Kent' —
he's on the British Overseas Trade Board for goodness' sake, and
the Duchess spends more time being a Samaritan and doing charity
work than she does being royal. Can he not pass the title over
to us? MC

P.P.S. I enclose some paint charts and fabric swatches to show
you what I have in mind for the Throne Room of our new home. MC

P.P.P.S. Does your cousin _really_ need Windsor Castle? After
all, she's got Buckingham Palace, Sandringham, Balmoral Castle,
Holyrood House. How many homes does the woman need, for
goodness' sake? I'm sure she wouldn't miss one tiny little
castle. See if we can have it, grace-and-favour. MC

P.P.P.P.S. I know British royalty always have corgis, but they
are not my choice of pet. Tell Lilibet that there will now be a
cat in the family. MC

From: Morag Auchtermuchty (Mrs)
      Refreshment Supervisor
      Licensed Victuallers Choir

**AUCHTERMUCHTY WHISKY DISTILLERY
WOOLLEN MILL & CAR REPAIR SERVICE
PERTHSHIRE, SCOTLAND**

3rd September 1990

Dear Connie,

Princess Michael of Kent, or Brunnhilde as they call her, has certainly
caused the Queen more than a few headaches over the last few years. Do you
remember the year when she set out on a horse down the Mall seconds before
the Queen was due to Troop the Colour? Her Majesty has ridden in a
carriage ever since. The Queen tries her best. She's offered the Michaels
the Governorship of the Maldive Islands, and she even suggested the
Princess for a part in 'Dallas', so what more could she do?

You can't help feeling sorry for the Royal Family, Connie, with not a
private moment to call their own. Look at the problems Prince Charles had
in finding a bride. Not many girls would take on a man without a proper
job and an uncertain future. I would have suggested Katriona, but she's
got too low a forehead for a tiara.

Your wee chum,
Morag

CONFIDENTIAL

Prospective Brides for His Royal Highness The Prince of Wales

(Girlfriends to date, 1979.)

Princess Marie Christina of the Netherlands

Princess Anne Marie of Denmark

Lady Caroline Percy

Lady Victoria Percy

Lady Julia Percy

Lady Georgina Petty-Fitzmaurice

Lucia Santa Cruz

Lady Leonora Grosvenor

'Tricia Nixon

Lady Jane Wellesley

Countess Angelika Lagansky

Barbra Streisand

Susan George

Fiona Watson

Jane Ward

Louise Astor

Georgiana Russell

Rosie Clifton

Sabrina Guinness

Anna Wallace

Princess Caroline of Monaco

Princess Marie-Astrid of Luxembourg

Amanda Knatchbull

Sybilla Dorman

The Buxton girls

Dale 'Kanga' Tryon

Lady Jane Grosvenor

Bettina Lindsay

Camilla Parker-Bowles

Lady Cecil Kerr

Lady Henrietta Fitzroy

Lady Charlotte Manner

Libby Manner

Angela Neville

Davina Sheffield

Lady Camilla Fane

Caroline Longman

Mother,
I seem to have dated every likely candidate; there's nobody left except Zsa-Zsa Gabor and Joan Collins.
What shall I do?
Charles

138

a good age to marry doesn't mean that you have to find someone this year. Just as long as you find someone before it's too late to father children. Have you thought about Selina Scott, that nice announcer we see on Grampian TV when we're at Balmoral? She's not married. Just three years younger than you. Perfect.

Forget about it for the time being. Accept Earl Spencer's invitation to Althorp. Johnny Spencer was one of my father's equerries, so you can go to Northampton, shoot, and put romance from your mind.

Mother

16th July 1979

Dear Mother,

I hope that the Buckingham Palace Garden Parties are going well this year and that you have not had too many crested teaspoons stolen. We've had a good hare shoot here and Earl Spencer has made us all very welcome. I hadn't realised that Raine Spencer's mother collaborated with Granny on books, but had wondered where Granny got the extra pocket money from for a few bets. At Ascot this year she had a bet on every horse in one race, so she was bound to win. Unfortunately her wardrobe is starting to suffer and she now seems to be wearing the same outfit every time I see her at Clarence House, so she'll have to write even more.

Mother, dear, I think I've fallen in love! Yes, I know what you'll say. I have thought this before, admittedly. One hundred and twenty-six times, to be precise. But this time it is for real, I can tell. It is Lady Sarah Spencer, a stunning redhead, who looks not unlike Selina Scott. Her first name is actually Elizabeth — how's that for a future Queen! — Elizabeth Sarah Lavinia Spencer, but she likes to be called Sarah. There's exactly the same age difference between us as there is between you and Father, so nobody could grumble about that. She's never been divorced, enjoys polo, and has actually fallen off a horse. So we have a lot in common. Sarah was practically born at Sandringham, too — at Park House, just two minutes' walk away.

Lady Sarah also has a younger sister who I saw trampling through the mud in Nobottle Wood (obviously trying to get a look at me) who is quite a jolly girl — Lady Diana. A little plain, but she'd make an excellent bridesmaid. What do you think?

Your son and heir,

Charles

I approve in principle but I only

know that her parents, Frances and Johnny (Philip and I were at the
wedding) are DIVORCED! Raine Spencer isn't really Sarah's mother,
just a step-mother. In fact, Raine divorced Gerald Legge, the
Earl of Dartmouth, to marry Johnny. My sister, my cousin, my uncle;
nobody in this family seems to be able to steer clear of divorce.
Thank goodness Anne and Mark's marriage is secure. I couldn't cope
with one of my own children divorcing. It would just be so
embarrassing.

I know that you have been acquainted with Lady Sarah for
several days now, but do not propose just yet. Invite her for a
weekend at Windsor first. We have to see if she is suitable.
I think the seventeen-course dinner test to begin with to see if she
knows which cutlery to use (one girl that you brought actually
used fish knives, remember - so middle class). Let's hope that
Lady Sarah passes the test.

Love,
Mother

WINDSOR CASTLE

27th July 1979

My dear Charles,

Having now met Lady Sarah Spencer, I think she is perfect for you. She and I had a long chat, Queen to commoner, over afternoon tea. I quizzed her about the family history and she knew instantly that the second Earl Spencer was Lord Privy Seal, the third was once Chancellor of the Exchequer, the fifth was Lord Lieutenant of Ireland, and so on. The very first Earl Spencer actually represented the Sovereign at the investiture of Frederick, Duke of Württemburg, as a Knight of the Garter at Stuttgart Cathedral in 1601. A rare honour. They must be one of the few families, though, who have started at the top and worked their way down. Bobo tells me that the present Earl is actually auctioning off paintings to pay for the upkeep of Althorp! Whatever next? Selling Althorp souvenirs, inviting paid guests to dinner, merchandising sticks of rock with Althorp all the way through? It doesn't bear thinking about. Bobo says that they actually have fake log fires! Is this true?

Anyway, Lady Sarah has a very British background, and the Spencers have a long association with our family, so I grant you permission to propose. What a weight it will be off my mind to have you settled, and no longer to have young actresses writing to me daily offering themselves as brides. I am arranging for a dinner service to be made as a wedding present for you, that will have the Spencer family arms on one side and your arms on the other.

Love,

Mother

BUCKINGHAM PALACE

28th July 1979

Dearest Mother,
Please forgive the writing, but I fell off my horse at polo this afternoon. Nothing too serious, just a bruised hand and a fractured fetlock. I shall be seeing Lady Sarah for a candlelit dinner in my suite, so hope to pop the question then. Andrew says I should invest in a toupée, one that would cover my ears, but I've decided that she must accept me just as I am.
Your son and heir,
Charles

CONNEM, ROBBEM & FLEECE

Estate Agents to the Aristocracy since 1872.

harpsichord room. Geographically convenient for a busy man
at just 90 minutes drive down the M4 from Buckingham Palace,
and even closer to Windsor. Handy for the Cheltenham Races,
Cirencester Polo Park, and within easy distance of the
Badminton Horse trials.

The property consists of:

FOUR Reception Rooms

NINE Main Bedrooms

SIX Bathrooms

BANQUET-SIZE Dining Room

KITCHEN

SERVANTS' Wing

NURSERY Wing - ideal for Princes/Princesses

STABLES - perfect for polo horses

ADJOINING Farm Buildings - one could grow one's own produce.

PRICE .... In region of £1,000,000 .... FREEHOLD

This superb property will be in great demand and should be
viewed at the earliest opportunity.

VIEWING BY APPOINTMENT THROUGH SOLE AGENTS

Let us arrange your mortgage!

143

BUCKINGHAM PALACE

1st August 1979

Dear Mother,

Sarah was not able to come for dinner as planned; it seems she had to meet someone important. The food was not wasted as her younger sister Diana, the one I told you about in the muddy field at Althorp, came along to tell me and I invited her to dinner instead. Diana is a very lively girl, and openly laughed at my record collection. I don't see what is funny about old Goon Show recordings, or the Band of the Royal Marines playing Jim Reeves, but there you are.

I'm considering buying a property in Gloucestershire. It's only ten miles from Gatcombe Park, so it would be ideal for Anne to keep an eye on the place whenever one is away.

Your son and heir,

Charles

Althorp House
Northamptonshire

2nd August, 1979.

My Dear Charles,
Before you go to Balmoral for six weeks I feel that I must write to you. I know that over the last few weeks you have become very attached to me. I have enjoyed our meetings and thank you for the video tape of the Coronation but I feel that I must be very honest with you and say that I like you very much as a Prince of Wales, I could even accept you as my Sovereign, but I could never have you as a husband. I know that you fall in love easily but I could never marry a man that I did not love and if you ask me I will have to turn you down. I am returning your Engagement Ring Size Chart and Westminster Abbey Seating Plan and hope that you will find a nice girl soon.

Affectionately,

Lady Sarah Spencer.

144

... ... wedding gift. If you married Diana
wouldn't have to have the Spencer family crest removed.
Just a thought. As so much investigation into the Spencers
has been done by the Secret Service it seems a shame to waste
all their time and effort, too.

Your ever loving

Mother

BUCKINGHAM PALACE

8th August 1979

Dear Mother,

Thank you for your letter and I will be coming up to Balmoral just as
soon as the repairs to Clarence House have been completed following Granny's
birthday party.

I like your suggestion about Lady Diana Spencer. As she is only eighteen
she has not had any past boyfriends either to compare me with, or who will sell
their stories to the newspapers. She has been registered with Knightsbridge
Nannies for a year now and in a few weeks' time begins work at the Young England
Kindergarten, so will make an excellent mother. I know that Andrew has his eye
on her and they are more of an age, so I must try and get in quick.

I do foresee one problem. Diana is much taller than I am; do you think
I should get my valet to order lifts for my shoes? I do know that Diana has
fallen off a horse, so we do have things in common.

Love, Charles

BALMORAL CASTLE

Lady Diana Spencer
60 Coleherne Court
Old Brompton Road
Earl's Court
London SW10

20 August 1980

My dear Diana,

I did so enjoy your stay here and was sorry when it came to
an end. I was sorry that you had to arrive after my sister
Anne's birthday and return before my Auntie Margaret's, but
I know that you would have felt embarrassed at being present
at such large family gatherings. I know you were sick with
nerves before having morning coffee with my mother. You
really don't have to be so shy, Diana. My mother thinks you
have a permanent stoop because you hide under your fringe.

I hope to come back to London early. I have been trying to
raise money to save the baboon. I have attempted to get the
money in the usual way, honestly. Now I'm going to see what
the Government can do.

I will telephone you at home, but will say that it's Baron
Renfrew (one of my other titles) and use one of my Goon
voices, so that your flatmates will not recognise me. In the
past when I've had a girlfriend the press has found out very
quickly and destroyed any chance of a relationship, but you
and I have really managed to keep them at bay this time.
Yippee!

Your Bonnie Prince,

Charles

21/VIII/80

'IN LOVE AGAIN'

Lady Diana Spencer is the new girl for Charles. It has
been revealed that Lady Di was seen fishing with the
Prince in the River Dee. She hid behind a pine tree each
time he cast his rod, but has been clearly identified. The
nineteen-year-old aristocrat, of impeccable breeding,
teaches at the Young England Kindergarten in Pimlico.
Among her charges is Diana Rigg's daughter Rachel.

146

O D E   T O   D I A N A

My knees to (royal) jelly turned, as when the lightning flashes.
So pray don't spurn me, beauteous maid, nor princely heart dishearten,
I'm putty in your hands, a child in lowly kindergarten.
O maid of Althorp, know you not my feelings grow intenser,
On you I see no blemishes, no taints, no marks, just Spencer.

O fairer far than Sarah, O blessed heaven-sent manna,
The Romans worshipped at your shrine, and so do I, Diana.
They raised you high, they knew you had one great divine ability -
It thrills my soul to know you were the goddess of fertility.
So think of me, where'er you be, Northamptonshire or Bali,
And know I'll be your slave (and King) and ever-loving Charlie.

* * * * * * * * * * *

16th September 1980

Dear Charles,

Help! My home and kindergarten are surrounded by press photographers. They poke their lenses through my letterbox, try and climb in the lavatory window. I was just going out to buy a new anorak from Peter Jones when I got trapped in a lift with a 'Sun' reporter. Fortunately he seemed unable to speak English and I was so tongue-tied and nervous that I couldn't say anything, so all was okay, but this is restricting my freedom, Charles. Seriously, yah?

I don't mind for myself, but my flatmates are beginning to suspect. Seriously. How can we try new dresses on in Selfridges with zoom lenses pointing at us?

Yours,

Diana

BUCKINGHAM PALACE

Dear Diana,

17th September 1980

Don't worry about the press. Ignore them and they'll just go away. That's what I do. Never say Di!

Today in a speech I said, and I thought it extremely profound, 'Eternity is so vast - who can comprehend it?'

'It's obvious you've never had a mortgage,' some bloke shouted from the back. Delightful.

I will be playing polo at Cowdray Park this weekend, if you would like to come, or if you prefer there is an open-air concert of 'Lucia Di Lammermoor' in Holland Park, which might be much more your cup of Earl Grey.

Your Bonnie Prince,

Charles

POST OFFICE
TELEGRAM 94
Service Instructions. Words.

No.
OFFICE STAMP
CONFIRMATION
LONDON W

= MUMMY STOP I HAVE BEEN GOING OUT WITH THE

PRINCE OF WALES RECENTLY STOP   I THINK HE IS

ABOUT TO ASK ME TO MARRY HIM STOP DIANA STOP =

LADY DIANA SPENCER + +

For free repetition of doubtful words telephone "TELEGRAMS ENQUIRY" or call, with this form   B or C
at office of delivery. Other enquiries should be accompanied by this form, and, if possible, the envelope

= DARLING DIANA STOP DON'T YOU THINK PRINCE

CHARLES IS TOO OLD TO BE ELIGIBLE? MUMMY STOP =

THE HON. FRANCES SHAND KYDD + +

For free repetition of doubtful words telephone "TELEGRAMS ENQUIRY" or call, with this form   B or C
at office of delivery. Other enquiries should be accompanied by this form, and, if possible, the envelope

= MUMMY STOP PRINCE CHARLES

IS TOO ELIGIBLE TO BE OLD STOP DIANA STOP =

LADY DIANA SPENCER + +

For free repetition of doubtful words telephone "TELEGRAMS ENQUIRY" or call, with this form
at office of delivery. Other enquiries should be accompanied by this form, and, if possible, the envelope   B or C

SANDRINGHAM HOUSE

16th January 1981

My dearest Diana,

Last night when you told me that you would be my Princess, you made me the happiest man alive. I hope you had a safe journey home and did not get backache lying on the floor of that Cortina, but we cannot let the press think that they have a scoop. I think my mother must like you as she has actually been outside and shouted at photographers. 'I wish you would all go away', she snapped. Then stalked back inside and said, 'I enjoyed that!' She was tempted to throw snowballs at them, but thought it might be a little undignified, so sent Anne out with Peter and Zara to do it instead. Anne is used to hurling things at the press.

I would like to make the news public now, but Mother says we have to give you time to change your mind. It is a big step to take and she insists that I must never get divorced. I am sure, my darling, but are you?

All my love,

Charles

POST   CARD

Coleherne Court
19th January 1981

My dear Charles,
    Of course I'm sure that I want to marry you!
Being Princess of Wales won't involve very much,
will it. I'll just be there in the background to
support you. A bit like a royal vicar's wife.
I know that the Press will leave me alone once
the honeymoon is over.
                        Luv ya,
                              Diana

151

BUCKINGHAM PALACE

My dearest Diana,

20th January 1980

Thank you for being so philosophical about it all.
Of course you are right. The novelty will soon wear off and
the press will leave you alone. I'm going off to Klosters on
my usual skiing holiday in three days' time. Perhaps you should
get away for a few days to think things over. Mother wants to
announce our engagement next month and as soon as that is done
Granny has offered you a room at Clarence House. She will be
able to give you lots of advice as she was Lady Elizabeth
Bowes-Lyon before her marriage, her father was an Earl (of
Strathmore), and she married a future King, so you and she have
much in common. I'm sure that the rent for the room will be
very reasonable, too.

I had dinner with Prince and Princess Michael of Kent at
Kensington Palace last evening. Princess Michael was telling me
about her latest overseas tour.

'First we went to Malaysia,' she said, 'then to Singapore,
which I loved, but China! Ah, the celestial Kingdom. I adored it
more than anything.'

'And did you see the pagodas?' I asked.

'Did we see them?' she glared. 'My dear, we had dinner with
them.'

Can you believe it!

I'll send you a postcard from Klosters, although it will be
signed 'Charlie Cornwall', one of my other titles.

All my love,
Charles

```
┌─────────────────────┐
│ LADY DIANA SPENCER  │
│ 60 COLEHERNE COURT  │
│ OLD BROMPTON ROAD   │
└─────────────────────┘
```

Luv,

Diana

BUCKINGHAM PALACE

* * *   24 February 1981   * * *   11.00 a.m.   * * *

It is with the greatest pleasure that The Queen and The Duke
of Edinburgh announce the betrothal of their beloved son, The
Prince of Wales, to the Lady Diana Spencer, daughter of the
Earl Spencer and the Honourable Mrs Shand Kydd.

HIGHGROVE HOUSE   25th February 1981

My dearest Diana

Now that we are at last engaged and you are safely in the care of my grandmother, I feel I ought to let you have just a few dates for your diary:

6th January	Epiphany Service	St James's Palace
Late March	Royal Film Performance	Odeon Cinema Leicester Sq.
Maundy Thurs.	Maundy Service	Cathedral in Britain
21st April	Mother's Birthday	Windsor Castle
Late May	Visit Chelsea Flower Show	Royal Hospital, Chelsea
End of May	Holyrood House Garden Parties	
Early June	Beating Retreat	Horse Guards Parade
13th June	Trooping the Colour	Horse Guards Parade
15th June	Garter Ceremony	Windsor Castle
June	Derby Day	Epsom Race Course
Mid-June	Ascot Races	Ascot Race Course
Mid-July	Royal Tournament	Earls Court
Late July	Buckingham Palace Garden Parties	
August	Family Holiday	Balmoral Castle
1st September	Highland Gathering	Braemar
4th November	State Opening of Parliament	Houses of Parliament
11th November	Remembrance Sunday + Festival of Remembrance on the Saturday evening	Cenotaph Royal Albert Hall
Late November	Royal Variety Show	London Palladium
December	Christmas with my family	Windsor Castle
New Year's Eve	Family Party (mine)	Sandringham House

Which year is this? Diana

Every year. Charles

Remember to keep these dates free.

All my love, Charles

154

CLARENCE HOUSE
S.W.1

[illegible]

[illegible], it disturbs the footmen', and 'Don't play pop music, it upsets the corgis'. On top of it all, I'm sure your mother doesn't like me. She even asked me who I was at the State Banquet last week.

'I thought I recognised your face', she said when I told her. Either she's jealous of the attention I'm getting or she has a very weird sense of humour.

Please, please, Charles. Can't I move into Buckingham Palace with you before the wedding? I'll go crazy here, with naps every afternoon after the racing and canasta in the evening. Is this what being royal is all about?

Help!

Diana

xx

BUCKINGHAM PALACE

4th March 1981

My dear Diana,

Thank you for your letter. Sorry you're having a rotten time, but you'll soon get used to Granny's little ways.

I'll be playing polo at Cowdray Park on Saturday afternoon, and have a Privy Council meeting in the early part of the evening, but if you'd like we can either go to the Poulenc concert at the Barbican or have dinner with mother at Windsor. You can choose.

I enclose a recipe for Nettle Tea, which will cure your nerves. Am just about to undertake engagements in Grimsby.

Yours,

Charles

CLARENCE HOUSE
S.W. 1

1st March 1981

My dear Charles,

While your grandmother has gone to present leeks to the Welsh Guards for St David's Day, I'm taking this opportunity to write to you. I'm not finding life here any easier. I had to play canasta with 'Arsenic and Old Lace' last night.

'How would you have played that last hand of mine?' I asked, hoping for advice from the Queen Mother.

'Under an assumed name,' she giggled.

Really, Charles, I wasn't that bad.

I feel that you are the only person I can turn to for advice who will not make me feel like a complete ignoramus. I'm launching my first ship tomorrow. How hard do I have to hit it to knock it into the water?

Your mother treats me like a simpleton and shouts at me as if she were talking to a foreigner. She wants my wedding dress to be made by the House of Hartnell or Hardie Amies and says she has plenty of material left over from her dress because so many clothing coupons were sent to her. I know the Royal Family likes continuity, but I want a fashionable designer dress. I don't want to look like Princess Anne.

The Lord Chamberlain has been going through the wedding preparations with me and I'm so confused. I don't know the Silver Stick Adjutant from the Gold Stick in Waiting, and how will I recognise all the guests? I don't know the Dowager Duchess of Abercorn from the Earl of Dalhousie. I just know that I shall make an absolute fool of myself. I wanted to have Wham! at the wedding but the Archbishop says I must have 'The Church's One Foundation' like everyone else. I think 'O God Our Help in Ages Past' would be more appropriate for me.

Oh, I told them that you want Kiri Te Kanawa to sing at the wedding. Is she one of your ex-girlfriends? She can sing while we're well out of the way signing the register in the vestry.

I'll see you at the State Banquet next week. I do hope that I am partnered with someone who can speak English this time.

All my love,

Diana
xxx

156

I had to give a speech at the Architects' Society last night. I've not
been enamoured with their designs of late so I said that they were a bunch of
blind, obstinate, unmitigated fools. They have made me an honorary member.

Princess Margaret told me a bit of gossip about the Kents last week.
Apparently Princess Michael returned from an engagement in a foul mood.

'Michael, you must dismiss our chauffeur,' she screamed. 'Five times now
he has almost killed me.'

'Please give the chauffeur another chance,' said Prince Michael in that
slow, deliberating way of his.

Princess Margaret laughed so much she nearly set fire to the sofa.

Don't worry about the wedding plans, my love. We employ people to do the
worrying for us. You will soon be a member of the Royal Family and have no
worries. My brother has sent me the following to give you:

'For your wedding you need - Something old (Queen Mother)

Something new (Diana)

Something borrowed (The jewellery)

Something blue (Princess Anne's language)'

All my love,
Charles

157

Menzies Toy Shop
Oban
Scotland

28th July 1981

Dear Diana,

Tomorrow you will walk down the aisle of St Paul's Cathedral in front of 50 million television viewers and will enter the history books as the ninth Princess of Wales. I must take this opportunity to send you my blessing and say that though you may become royal, you're still my little girl. I will be there on your wedding day, although fortunately it's been arranged that I will share a carriage with Prince Philip so won't have to travel with your father. So if you forget your words just look at me and I'll mouth them to you. I've been through it twice, remember.

I trust that 'Acid Raine' hasn't been invited. I've never forgiven her for saying that you were brainless and thought that Afghanistan was a type of cheese. If you were brainless you wouldn't have got the most eligible bachelor in the world, so think on. Thank goodness you stood up for yourself and told her that Afghanistan is a type of wool. I assume that Barbara Cartland hasn't been invited either. They couldn't have anyone upstaging the Queen Mother in the feathers and chiffon department.

Now, Diana, as your mother I feel I must be frank. Your stepfather likes it that way. I know that the pressure is on Prince Charles to have a son and heir, but don't let him force you into anything that you aren't ready for. If he looks amorous, lock the connecting door between your two bedrooms. If it's too late, then here

e) In a minute, but I must just go downstairs for another pickled onion first.

f) Have you seen Lady Tryon lately?

g) You know I haven't got my gold American Express card.

h) Is it a trick of the light, or is your bald spot getting bigger?

All these are guaranteed to cool his ardour. But just to make sure, you could always stand a photograph of your stepmother on the bedside table.

Be happy, Diana, and don't let your new life change you. Don't let them force you into growing your hair long so that you can wear a tiara (if it doesn't suit you), don't be talked into having a corgi (it'll shed hair all over your Axminster), and don't let them get you up on a horse (you're too slim to wear jodhpurs).

Love,

Mother

HOW ROMANTIC IS YOUR LOVER?

Has your long-term relationship lost its initial sparkle, or is the flame of passion still very much alight? In an age of sex equality does your partner still believe in old-fashioned romanticism? LAVINIA BOLTON-PICKLES-SMITH asks the questions.

1 **How often does your partner suggest you eat out?**
a Several times a week? ✓
b Once a month?
c Twice a year?

We never eat in.

2 **Do you share the housework?**
a Never? ✓
b Sometimes?
c Always?

We don't have to do it.

3 **If your partner were to buy you a ring, what stone would it be?**
a Diamond? ✓ *Ruby, Sapphire, Emerald, Opal etc*
b Semi-precious?
c Costume fake?

4 **Do you know your partner's most erogenous zone?**
a Ears? ✓✓✓
b Shoulders?
c Feet?

5 **When you go on holiday, does your partner suggest:**
a A romantic castle? ✓ *Always*
b A three-star hotel?
c A self-catering holiday chalet in Grimsby?

b Only on Saturday nights?
c He hasn't said it since 1963?

8 **When your partner sees you naked, does he/she say:**
a 'You are as gorgeous as Diana/Adonis'? ✓ *I am Diana!*
b 'The F-Plan diet isn't working'?
c 'Move over, your bum's blocking the telly'?

9 **If you were to win a million pounds, would your partner:**
a Not want it to change your lifestyle? ✓ *It wouldn't change our lifestyle*
b Insist it changed your lifestyle?
c Drink it all away?

10 **When you spend a quiet evening in front of the television, do you:**
a Watch the soaps and hold hands? ✓ *and old coronation films*
b Watch in separate rooms?
c Never watch because you cannot agree on the channel?

How does your partner rate?

If you ticked mostly **a** s, *I am!*
what a romantic softy you have. You must be treated like royalty.
If you ticked mostly **b** s,
your partner is probably having an affair.
If you ticked mostly **c** s,
you are a fool and should have ditched the pig years ago.

T H E   R O U T E   T O

P R I N C E   A N D R E W ' S   B E D R O O M

1) Sneak in through Privy Purse Door. (Say you've come to sign the Visitor's Book. Nobody does these days, so by the time they find it, you can be in.)

2) Go down the Privy Purse Corridor, but do not use the Queen's Lift - it creaks.

3) Take first corridor on left, through the Marble Hall and up the Grand Staircase. The family never use it, only guests, so you'll be alright.

4) Once up the stairs go through the Picture Gallery. Don't use the Household Corridor: the staff hear everything. Tiptoe past the Queen's Dining Room, Study, Bedroom and Dressing Room, preferably on a night when Her Majesty is at Windsor.

5) Go down the King's Corridor, where you'll find another staircase. Up that to the top floor. Turn right and my room is at the end of the corridor. No need to knock, the door is always open.

I   W I L L   B E   W A I T I N G !

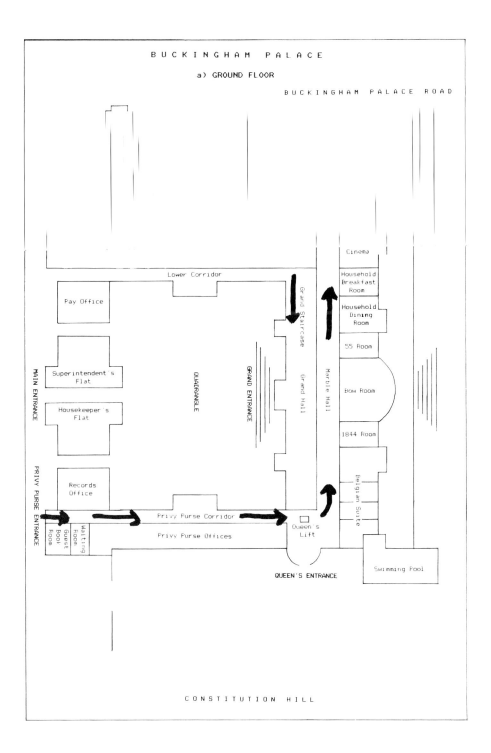

BUCKINGHAM PALACE

a) GROUND FLOOR

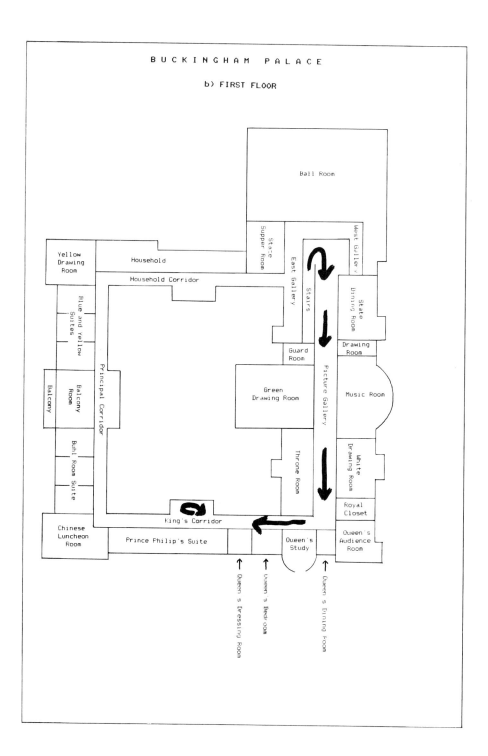

B U C K I N G H A M   P A L A C E

b) FIRST FLOOR

Ball Room

State Supper Room

West Gallery

Yellow Drawing Room

Household

East Gallery

State Dining Room

Household Corridor

Stairs

Blue and Yellow Suites

Drawing Room

Principal Corridor

Guard Room

Balcony

Balcony Room

Green Drawing Room

Picture Gallery

Music Room

Buhl Room Suite

Throne Room

White Drawing Room

Royal Closet

King's Corridor

Chinese Luncheon Room

Prince Philip's Suite

Queen's Study

Queen's Audience Room

Queen's Dressing Room

Queen's Bedroom

Queen's Dining Room

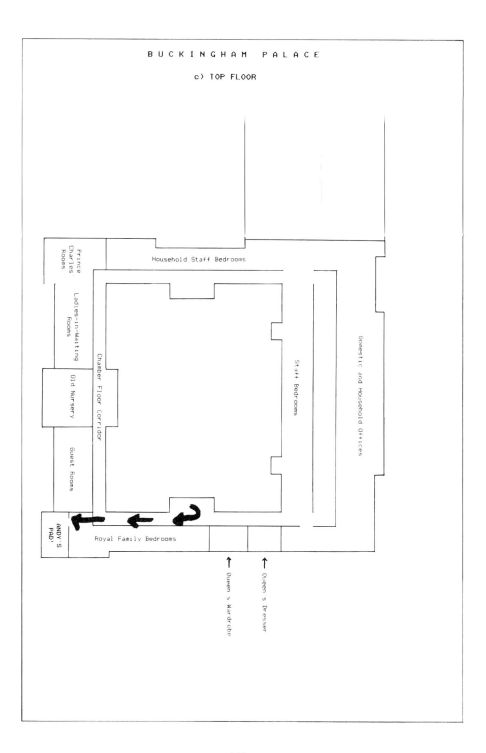

DUMMER DOWN FARM

DUMMER, BASINGSTOKE, HAMPSHIRE

20th June 1985

Dear Prince Andrew,

What a scream it was at Ascot yesterday, although I don't think your mother was too pleased when we threw profiteroles at each other, but what a hoot! I thought the press might have picked it up, but then my father is your brother's polo manager, and as jounalists haven't got the foggiest idea what the game is all about, we Fergusons just get ignored. I suppose if Daddy went to a Soho massage parlour or something it might cause a stir, but I expect our day-to-day lives are just too ordinary. Sorry if I thumped Diana in the ribs too hard - I know she was winded for a moment, but she really was being the most frightful bore. Going on and on about Jasper Cunran and Bruce Oldfield. I looked through the programme, but I couldn't see whether they were the horses or the jockeys. Certainly I didn't hear that either of them had won.

If you can delay going back to sea a bit longer, perhaps you can come abseiling with me at the weekend? Only down the north face of Portsmouth Town Hall, but there aren't many mountains in Hampshire, what!

Toodle pip!　(as my father says.　Or is it your
mother to Prince Philip!!!).

Sarah

BUCKINGHAM PALACE　　21st June 1985,

Dear Fergie-Burger,
I thought we might do something a bit less energetic at the weekend. I've got two tickets for a film called Emily. It stars a friend of mine, Katharine Steak, and I assume it's by Charlotte Brontë.

Where did you get the exploding envelopes from? What a wheeze!

Yours, Randy Andy

...joyed the film 'Emily', but it was a bit low-budget. They obviously couldn't afford many costumes, but you'd think that they could at least have found a man to play the love scene instead of having to use two actresses. Even I know two women can't have a baby, so it wasn't very convincing.

Diana's kindly given me some of her old clothes. Gosh, she's worn them twice and one of them three times, so they're really of no use to her. It was a kind gesture on her part, but it's involving a lot of work for me trying to match up the materials to put a yard or two in the seams. I've found that in the end, it's much easier to have the dresses cut up horizontally, then two or three can be joined together. Neat, eh?

I shall miss you when you go back on to HMS Brazen but a friend of mine has her own private plane, so perhaps I can parachute in for tea? In fact, one of my evening dresses, the one which you squirted with raspberry sauce although nobody noticed, is actually made from parachute silk. Had a postcard from Kim Bingham-Smith today and an invitation to a sporting weekend with Paddy McNally. Dear Andrew, I do hope that you don't mind the fact that I've had boyfriends in the past? Does it worry you?

I hope to go Bunjie diving next week. You jump off a bridge tied to a piece of elastic, wow!

Take care, chucklebum.

Fergie

ATTN: SARAH FERGUSON

DEAREST FERGIE-POOS,
GLAD YOU ENJOYED YOUR BUNJIE DIVING AND HOPE THAT THE REPAIRS TO THE
BRIDGE DON'T COST THE DEPARTMENT OF THE ENVIRONMENT TOO MUCH MONEY.
I KNOW IT'S TIME FOR THE WINDOWS OF BUCKINGHAM PALACE TO BE CLEANED
AGAIN AND MOTHER GETS VERY UPSET IF THE DEPARTMENT'S BUDGET HAS RUN
OUT.

I SHALL MISS YOU WHILE I'M AWAY, BUT HOPE TO POP BACK FOR THE QUEEN
MOTHER'S BIRTHDAY (4TH AUGUST), THE GHILLIES' BALL AT BALMORAL (19TH
AUGUST), THE BRAEMAR HIGHLAND GATHERING (1ST SEPTEMBER), REMEMBRANCE
SUNDAY (11TH NOVEMBER), CHRISTMAS AT WINDSOR AND NEW YEAR AT
SANDRINGHAM, SO HOPE TO SEE SOMETHING OF YOU. WHY DON'T YOU GO SKIING
WITH CHARLES AND DIANA IN JANUARY, AND WE'LL MEET UP IN FEBRUARY?

GUY ROXBURGHE HAS INVITED ME UP TO SCOTLAND FOR A WEEKEND AND I USUALLY
TAKE A FRIEND. WILL YOU COME? YOU'LL LOVE STAYING AT FLOORS CASTLE IN
KELSO AS GUY LET IT BE USED AS THE SET OF 'GREYSTOKE', THE TARZAN FILM.
I KNOW THAT YOU ENJOY DOING TARZAN IMPRESSIONS.

LOOK AFTER YOURSELF WHILE I'M AWAY. I HOPE YOUR WORK AT THE
PUBLISHER'S IS GOING WELL. ALTHOUGH MY LAST BOOK HAS BEEN REMAINDERED,
I WOULD LOVE TO DO A SECOND, BUT WHERE WOULD I FIND A PUBLISHER TO TAKE
IT ON?

LOVE,
ANDY-POOS.

39584 HMSBRZ G
73920 BCKGRA G
*

POST   CARD

Up Snowdon.
(No, not Princess Margaret's ex-husband!)
Dearest Andy-Poos,
    Just a card to let you know that I am
keeping busy while you are away. I'm staying
with friends in Wales. We were up a mountain
the other day and the chair-lift broke down.
I managed to give it a push-start, but found
myself flying through the air like someone in
a James Bond movie. Great fun.
    I'm trying it again today!

                    Fergie
                      x
                    x x

Snowdon in rain.

168

Her Majesty the Queen,

well, I have asked her to marry me, I know

this will come as a shock to you, but you did not
approve of Koo Stark, Vicki Hodge, Katie Rabbett, et
al, and I don't want to be as old as Charles before
I find a wife and settle down. Sarah may be a
commoner, but then so is Diana. However, she can
trace her ancestry back to King Charles II and
Robert the Bruce of Scotland, and her grandmother
is a cousin of the Duchess of Gloucester.

Please, please, please, Mum, say yes. Sarah will
be so upset if you don't agree; already she is
going around singing 'Some Day My Prince Will
Come', and there aren't any royal weddings
planned for this year are there?

Love,

Andrew.

P.S. Could you send me a few pounds to help buy a
ring? Navy pay doesn't go very far, you know.

BUCKINGHAM PALACE

6th February, 1985.

(33rd anniversary of my
accession and you didn't send a card.)

Dear Andrew,

I have nothing against Sarah Ferguson in principle, and certainly
she has the effect of making Diana look very dignified, but her parents
have been DIVORCED! How can I possibly make Margaret feel guilty, when my
entire family seems tainted by dissolution? My sister, my daughter-in-law,
my cousin, my uncle; all around me there are problems.

As an example of what divorce can do, just look at an extract from a
letter I had today from a distraught man in Berkhamsted:

'Your Majesty,

I married a divorcée who had a grown-up daughter. My father
fell in love with my stepdaughter and married her. So, he became my
son-in-law and my stepdaughter became my stepmother (as my father's
wife).

My wife and I had a son, who is now my father's brother-in-law,
and also my uncle because he is the brother of my stepmother.
My stepmother had a son, who is my brother, but also my grandchild
because he is the son of my stepdaughter.

Now I realise that my wife must be my grandmother because she
was my father's mother, which makes me my wife's husband and
grandchild at the same time, and as the husband of a person's
grandmother, I am now my own grandfather!

I am suicidal, Ma'am, what can I do?'

Now, Andrew, do you see the problems of divorce? If I'd let Margaret
marry Peter Townsend, she'd probably be my step-Mistress of the Robes or
something.

That apart, I agree to your betrothal, but must make the following
provisos:

1/ Sarah is not to do her Margaret Rutherford impressions in public.

2/ She is not to wear anything that will upstage Diana.

3/ Under no circumstances is she to put whoopee cushions under my chair [illegible]

[illegible] my balcony.

7/ I will not allow profiteroles at the wedding breakfast; we never could remove that chocolate stain.

8/ You will accept the title Duke of York on your wedding day as my gift; I cannot possibly have Sarah called Princess Andrew, as people might think she was on a par with Princess Michael.

Your loving,

Mother

BUCKINGHAM PALACE

* * * 19 March 1986 * * * 11.00 a.m. * * *

It is with the greatest trepidation that Her Majesty The Queen and the Duke of Edinburgh announce the engagement of their son, The Prince Andrew, to Miss Sarah Ferguson, ex-Head Girl of Hurst Lodge School and jolly good sport, daughter of Major Ronald Ferguson and Mrs Susan Barrantes (divorced).

From: Morag Auchtermuchty (Mrs)
      Lead Soprano Licensed Victuallers Choir

12th September 1990

Dear Connie,

   Sorry I haven't been in touch, but I've been doing a few gigs with the choir. The tour covered all the top venues in Killiecrankie, Dornock and Frisby-on-the-Wreak, and it seemed to be successful. Especially my solo, 'Oh, I Wish I Were A Tiny Little Bird'. 'More like a bloody great buzzard,' some man shouted from the back of the hall.

   'I'll have you know I'm a coloratura,' I shouted.

   'I don't care what your religion is, but ye cannae sing,' he replied.

   Well, Connie, I've been trying to find the love letters of Prince Edward, but there seems to be no evidence that he's ever been in love. Unless you count his work. I expect that as he has such an ordinary job he can openly have girlfriends without being noticed. I read in the gutter press that he might be gay! Good Heavens, Connie! I know they say 'one in four' and Her Majesty has four children, but he's been in the Royal Marines, so he can't be. I'm sure that the only queens in his life are all blue-blooded royals. One thing, he's so rude to my Katriona that I can easily see a romance blossoming there. What do you think I should wear as mother of the bride? I don't want to clash with the Queen on the balcony.

   Please find enclosed one of the most historic letters of all. This could be our future Queen, Connie.

Your wee chum,

Morag

says they are funnier than Goon Shows, whatever they are. My father
I know I am younger than you, but you are not married and
neither am I, so how would you like to be Queen of England one
day? I've got a big poster of you in my bedroom. I'm going to
make lots of changes when I am King. I shall have vitamins and
iron put in ice cream, sweets and chocolate cake instead of
spinach and carrots. I shall change the National Anthem to 'I
Should Be So Lucky. Lucky, Lucky, Lucky', one of your greatest
hits.

My Auntie Sarah and Uncle Andrew were going to take me to see
one of your films, but Granny wouldn't let them because you don't
speak the Queen's English and Maoris throw eggs and wet t-shirts
at her whenever she visits your part of the world. Auntie Sarah
and Uncle Andrew gave me a drum to play with instead. After a
while Grandpa Philip gave me a penknife so I could see what is in
the middle of the drum.

When I came home from school the other day my mother said,
'What has Mummy's little Prince learned this afternoon?' I said
I learned two kids not to call me 'Mummy's little Prince'.

Well, think about my offer. You won't get a better one. It
could be a whole new dynasty (Mummy's favourite programme) and
we'll become the House of Mountbatten-Minogue-Windsor. Must go
as this is Papa's word processor and I could be forced to pay
some pocket money for the floppy disc.

Keep singing, Kylie. My Papa says that you are not without
lack of talent and manage to sing even the simplest songs with
the greatest strain, so that must be good. He even said that
you're not brilliant but mediocre!

            With regal greetings,

                    Prince William of Wales
                            xx

1O DOWNING STREET

13 September 1990

Dear Lady Crabtree,

I know that the general public will be delighted by your latest discoveries, and certainly it will take their minds off the interest rates and Community Charge.

I hope that one day you will be able to reveal some of our bedtime secrets. Only last week I was told by the armed security man who stands outside our door that in his sleep Denis, who loves golf as you know, shouted 'Fore!' I apparently shouted 'Four and a quarter!' Obviously dreaming about inflation again.

Denis and I celebrate our Ruby Wedding Anniversary in 1991 and if it happens to coincide with the General Election I think a few revelations from our love letters could well influence the voters.

Your desire to be made a Dame Grand Cross of the Royal Victorian Order has been noted, but I am afraid this honour is the Queen's prerogative and therefore out of my hands.

Yours sincerely,

Margaret.

The Rt. Hon. Mrs Margaret Thatcher PM

The Dowager Lady Crabtree

The Secret Journals of Queen Elizabeth II

Now read, in Virgin paperback, the original diaries first brought to the public eye by Constance, Lady Crabtree. Revealing

The Secret Journals of
Queen Elizabeth II

Edited by
Constance, Lady Crabtree

£4.99 in Virgin paperback, from all good bookshops, or direct from the publisher.

Virgin Books
W. H. Allen & Co Plc
26 Grand Union Centre
338 Ladbroke Grove
London W10 5AH

ISBN 0-86369-393-8